D1475354

THEY PERSISTED

MARGARET M KIRK

Margaret M. Kirk

COPYRIGHT

Second Edition

Edited by **Laura J Martin**

Cover Photo Credit: *Chicago Tribune*, June 6, 1916

Library of Congress Control number 2017917618

ISBN – 979-8-3507-0111-1 (print)

ISBN – 979-8-05881-4 (eBook)

DEDICATION

This book is dedicated with deep admiration and gratitude to Barb Macraz, who first encouraged me to write this book. She said something like, I see a book, you should put a book together, those women need a book to tell their stories. Of course, Barb has done amazing work establishing and filling libraries in Morocco and in thirty schools and community sites. She most likely sees books everywhere. She also works tirelessly to protect elephants and other endangered wildlife with her nonprofit, The Oliveseed Foundation. They are doing great community-led work in Kenya. This woman is a true inspiration. She persists – always, and perhaps we need a book about her! Thank you, Barb

TABLE OF CONTENTS

ACKNOWLEDGEMENTS

Deep gratitude to Laurie Martin, my soul sister with an eagle eye, who edited this second edition. I am not certain I would have had the ability or fortitude to continue without her brilliance.

A huge debt of gratitude to:

Dana Petersen, Patty Harpham, and Shari Dunn for their encouragement and support.

A'lelia Bundles, author, journalist, speaker, great-great-granddaughter, and biographer of Madam C.J. Walker, for generously giving her time, expertise, and family history.

Ara Campbell, Shelly Vermilya, Ed.D, and Dr. Kat Quina for reading the manuscript and offering their comments and support.

Phyllis Hollenbeck, Pat Shepherd, the Mancos Public Library, Rhonda Schaefer at San Juan College, Lisa Marine at the Wisconsin Historical Society, the San Diego Zoo, the Amon Carter Museum, the Archivists at Smith College, the U.S. Coast Guard, the San Diego Historical Society, and always Dr. Michelle Hemingway and to *all* the women who persist!

INTRODUCTION

"Each time a girl opens a book and reads a womanless history, she learns that she is worth less." Myra Pollack Sadker

History connects us, like the threads that create a tapestry, stitching us securely into a multigenerational quilt of life and community. History helps us learn who we are. When we don't know our own history, our power and dreams are inherently diminished. History must tell the whole story.

It is likely that you already know about some interesting women in history, like Eleanor Roosevelt, Rosa Parks, and Amelia Earhart, to name a few. However, there are so many more amazing women that you may not have heard about, like Helen Marot, Mary Fields, Bessie Coleman, and others. Knowing the achievements of women expands our sense of what is real and what is possible.

In 1999, shortly before the Ken Burns documentary, "Not for Ourselves Alone: The Story of Elizabeth Cady Stanton and Susan B. Anthony" was produced, a survey was done by General Motors, who was going to sponsor the film. They wanted to see how many people knew who these women were. These two women helped transform a nation! The very sad and very disturbing result was that fewer than one percent could identify either woman as being connected to women's rights.

Women's history is, by its very nature, political. By understanding the differences in gender over time, we can better respond to those who tell us how men and women "should" act, live, or feel. What is needed is a historical consciousness. A *complete* history helps us to find that consciousness.

It is my intent to inspire and encourage anyone of any age, particularly young women, that the sky's the limit. That despite obstacles, real or imagined, with enough passion, hard work, and determination, you can accomplish anything!

I have made every effort to ensure that the information presented is factual, and without error, using reliable sources; academic whenever possible. However, these women lived long ago, in a time where information gathering and preservation may have been unreliable, and there is much on the internet that lacks validity. My intention has been to present as honest a picture of these women as possible.

This collection of stories lifts twenty-one women up who have been relegated to the archives, where they have become fossilized and dusty. It breathes new life into them. They are vessels for preserving the truth and inspiring a new generation. I hope you enjoy getting to know these women as much as I did!

Some suggestions for further reading are at the end of the chapters.

Ann Preston

"...while to a large portion of things and observing men, the medical education of women appears to be the natural result of the progress of society, there are others who still regard it as some abnormal social phenomenon; some abrupt and fantastic freak of unbridled liberty, unfitted to stand the test of time and experience."

Ann Preston was born on December 1, 1813, in West Grove, Pennsylvania, to a prosperous farmer, Amos Preston, and his wife Margaret Smith Preston. They were a family of Quaker abolitionists. The family farm, Prestonville, was well known as a safe harbor for runaway slaves. Quakers were among the first white people to denounce slavery in the American Colonies and Europe. The Society of Friends became the first organization to take a collective stand against both slavery and the slave trade, later spearheading international and ecumenical campaigns against slavery. In 1776, Quakers were prohibited from owning slaves, and fourteen years later, they petitioned the United States Congress for the abolition of slavery. (A primary Quaker belief is that all human beings are equal and worthy of respect. The fight for human rights has also extended to many other areas of society).

Ann's early education was at the Westtown Quaker School in West Chester, Pennsylvania. When her mother fell ill, Ann was forced to return home to care for her younger siblings. She had two sisters, but one died in infancy and the other in her early years. All six of her brothers survived.

Ann was very active in the Clarkson Anti-Slavery Society, temperance, and women's rights movements. She attended lectures at the local lyceum and belonged to a literary society. She published a book of nursery rhymes titled *Cousin Ann's Stories*. It was during this time in Ann's young life she discovered, much to her dismay, just how boring and sedentary the lives of many women were.

Ann also noted even women's clothing was uncomfortable and painfully restrictive. She felt women needed outside activity, education, and a better understanding of their own physiology and hygiene. This was a time of awakening and decision-making for her. She sought out a Quaker physician, Dr. Nathanial R. Moseley, who took her on as an apprentice in July 1847. The apprenticeship lasted two years. As her siblings grew older and became more independent, Ann had more time to dedicate to her passions. She taught all-female classes in physiology, health, and hygiene.

In 1849, upon completion of her apprenticeship with Dr. Mosley, Ann applied to four medical colleges in Pennsylvania. They rejected her at all four colleges because of her gender. In May 1849, *The National Era* reported that Elizabeth Blackwell graduated from medical school. "Some of our male readers may be astonished to see an M.D. attached to the name of one of the gentler sex," the editors wrote, "but we hope the time will come when an American woman, at least, can follow any honorable professional occupation… without exciting the surprise of anyone." Ann felt the same way and may have been inspired by Blackwell's words. Her course was set, and her focus was clear. She would become a physician and she would help pave the way for her students who wished to do the same.

In 1850, a group of Quakers founded the Female Medical College of Pennsylvania, later changed to the Woman's Medical College of Pennsylvania (WMCP). There were now many women seeking a profession in medicine, and this would help facilitate their needs. Ann enrolled in the first class, along with seven other women. While a student there, she wrote to her dear friend, Hannah Darlington: "The joy of exploring a new field of knowledge, the rest from accustomed pursuits and cares, the stimulus of completion, the novelty of a new kind of life, are all mine, and all for the time possess a charm. And then, I am restful in spirit and well satisfied that I came."

After graduating, Ann stayed at the school for another year of postgraduate study. Upon completion, she was appointed professor of physiology and hygiene at the college. She was thirty-eight years old.

Ann campaigned vigorously for her female students to attend clinical lectures at the Blockley Philadelphia Hospital and the Pennsylvania Hospital. She negotiated the very best learning environment and educational opportunities for them, despite the often-open hostility of both male medical students and male faculty members. One might have expected better of the faculty, but patriarchy has deep roots.

In 1858, the medical field was predominantly male. The Philadelphia Medical Society spoke out against the Woman's Medical College, prohibiting women from all medical societies and studying in medical clinics. The faculty, however, could not seem to find a way to best address the issue of the education of women in medicine. They wished it would just go away! That would not happen. Dr. Preston rose to the occasion and organized an advisory board of "lady managers." Most were wealthy and influential supporters of women in medicine and raised a collective voice, as well as the funds, to establish and run a hospital where students would have excellent and easy access to clinical experience for critical hands-on training. The new hospital opened in 1861. In 1863, Ann established a nursing school on site, one of the first institutions to do so in the United States.

Women in medicine were making some progress, but there was still a long way to go. In an introductory lecture to her students, Ann stated: "while to a large portion of thinking and observing men, the medical education of women appears to be the natural result of the progress of society, there are others who still regard it as some abnormal social phenomenon; some abrupt and fantastic freak of unbridled liberty, unfitted to stand the test of time and experience." Change never seems to come easily.

Dr. Ann Preston became dean of the Woman's Medical College in 1866, the first woman dean of an American medical school. A year later, they elected Ann to the governing board. When the college opened its doors, there were only three women doctors on the faculty and twenty students enrolled. It was a quality institution and soon grew and prospered. It was not long before many eminent physicians, male, and female, were among the teaching staff. Ann's hard work and determination were paying off.

Once again, Ann was clear, focused, and determined to improve access to clinical and other educational opportunities for her students, despite the pushback and open hostility of some practitioners and other educators. Dr. Preston negotiated with Philadelphia Hospital to allow her students to attend the general clinics conducted there. In 1869, she made similar arrangements with Pennsylvania Hospital, but her students were constantly and mercilessly harassed by male students. Ann accompanied her women students, the women physicians in training, to the first clinic. There, she witnessed first-hand the drama that unfolded. The men shouted insults at the women and threw spitballs and tobacco quids - a mixture of tobacco, crushed areca nuts (also called betel nuts), spices, and other ingredients. The betel nut is used like chewing tobacco, placed in the mouth between the gum and cheek). Some even spit sour tobacco juice on their clothing. But the women students were determined, remained composed, and kept up their attendance at clinics, even though they were also occasionally pelted with rocks as they left by the back door. Yes, the back door. The front door was only for the men. Over the next ten years, the number of female doctors in America rose by thirty-four percent. By 1880, over 2,400 women were practicing medicine in America. It was a time of change for women and society, a change that did not come easily.

On February 21, 1925, Ann wrote to a former student, Sarah C. Hall, recalling the events of the early days. The occasion was the 75th anniversary of the Woman's Medical College. "We were allowed to enter by way of the back stairs and were greeted by the male students with hisses and paper wads, and frequently during the clinic were treated to more of the same. The professor of surgery came in and bowed to the men only. More hisses... We retired the same way we entered and on reaching the outer door, found male students lined up on one side of the way, and we, to get out, had to take the road and walk to the street to the tune of 'The Rogues March.' (Rogues March was a derisive piece of music that was developed to shame delinquent soldiers, to punish them for their transgressions, a nasty taunt song). Our students separated as soon as possible and all who could rode the little, antiquated horse cars in any direction they were going. The men separated also, and in groups of twos, threes and fours followed the women."

Under the leadership and guidance of Dr. Ann Preston, the Woman's Medical College (WMCP) graduated several firsts. Some of these outstanding women were Mary Putnam Jacobi, the leading American woman medical scientist of the nineteenth century; Clara Swain, the first woman medical missionary, traveling to India in 1869; Anna Broomall, a master teacher of obstetrics who created an early program of prenatal visits, and Catharine Macfarlane, who conducted the first study in preventing pelvic cancers. WMCP always claimed a diverse student body, inclusive regardless of race, ethnicity, or religion. It graduated some of the earliest African American women doctors, including Rebecca Lee Crumpler, Eliza Grier, and Matilda Evans; the first Indian woman doctor, Anandibai Joshee; the first Native American woman doctor, Susan Laflèche Picotte; and other women M.D.s from China, Syria, and South America.

The college admitted Jewish students in the nineteenth century--earlier than many other medical schools--reflective of the growing Jewish immigrant community in South Philadelphia. In the mid-1940s, the school accepted five Japanese American students, at least three of whom had been imprisoned in internment camps. Another of the women graduating from WMCP was Sarah Mapps Douglass, an African American teacher, abolitionist, writer, artist, and public lecturer - and a Quaker. Some students audited the courses and returned to their communities to give women the advantage of the knowledge they had gained in physiology and hygiene. Most of the women they worked with were the poorest of the poor. They were pioneering medical outreach as a branch of social work. This is quite a collection of very impressive women!

Not only was Ann a physician, teacher, and advocate, she was an extraordinary fundraiser. The school needed capital to keep running. Ann raised sufficient funds to send her close friend and colleague, Dr. Emmeline Horton Cleveland to Paris, to study obstetrics. When Emmeline returned home, she would become a resident physician at the newly established hospital. Why go to Paris? Paris, at this point in history, was delivering obstetrics into a new and more enlightened era. Maternal mortality was a staggering thirteen times higher in hospital births than in home births. Puerperal fever and perinatal uterine infection ran rampant. It was concluded that infections were being transmitted throughout the hospital via unwashed hands and shared linens. When new hygienic practices were instituted, maternal mortality was dramatically reduced. Forceps were designed to ease birth, especially breech births, which were previously manually manipulated, but not always successfully. There were cutting-edge practices being developed in Paris.

When money was slow to come in, Ann would borrow her family's horse and buggy, going door to door and farm to farm in Chester, Bucks, and Montgomery counties, pleading her case and urging Quaker families to be generous in their giving. The Woman's Medical College had high standards, and soon not only survived, but it thrived, becoming famous as a prestigious teaching institution. The college also trained and sent the first women medical missionaries to Asia.

In her later years, Ann suffered from a rheumatic condition. However, she persisted as a professor of physiology and consulting physician at the college. Her private practice dwindled, as it was too painful for her to ride to visit patients in their homes.

Ann had a vision, and she made it a reality. She fought narrow-mindedness with vigilance, saying that women were patients, and it was "in accordance with the instincts of the truest womanhood for women to appear as physicians and students."

As recently as 1948, the following appeared in a *New York Post* article. "Do Women Make Good Doctors?" Noting the continuing rejection of female doctors by their male colleagues, the article reported the "amusingly transparent" tricks used by some male doctors to keep women out of their specialties. "The New York Obstetrical Society... in spite of the nature of its specialty, does not admit women physicians to membership... because the society holds its meetings in the Yale Club, through whose sacred portals no women may enter." Boston's Obstetrical Society didn't have this limitation to its meetings; the organization simply didn't elect women. "Even a great many maternity hospitals do not have women doctors on their staff."

Suggestions for further reading:

Send Us a Lady Physician: Women Doctors in America, 1850–1920 by Ruth J. Abram

History of the Woman's Medical College, Philadelphia, Pennsylvania, 1850–1950 by Gulielma Fell Alsop

Belle Jennings Benchley

Photo Credit: San Diego Historical Society

"...a soft word instead of a club, a gentle twinkle of the eye instead of a whip."

Belle Jennings was born on August 28, 1882, in Larned, Kansas, to Frederick Merritt Jennings and

Jane Orrell Jennings. Jane came to southern Illinois with Frederick, who was a famous blacksmith. He created carriages and other necessary implements, displaying great craftsmanship and artistry. Jane's paternal grandfather was Austin Hilton Jennings, one of the first settlers in Ohio, and one of the founders of Ohio Wesleyan University. Austin held life scholarships at that institution to educate all thirteen of his children. He valued education and wanted his children to have access to the best. Austin and his wife began their married life in a log cabin with dirt floors and oiled paper windows. He wanted more for his offspring, and he knew education was key.

Frederick and Jane had eight children. Belle was the second oldest. When she was five, the family moved to California, staying in Los Angeles for a few months, before moving to San Diego County, where Belle's father became the sheriff. They settled in the Roseville area of Point Loma, and Belle wandered the beaches and hills with her younger siblings.

During this time, Belle developed a deep and lasting love and respect for animals. She also became an expert at identifying flowers, birds, and shells. Belle's early education, along with her siblings, was at the Roosevelt School. This was in the Jennings home, as there was no room for it in the town. Belle later attended Russ High School and then graduated from San Diego Teachers College in 1902.

After her graduation from college, Belle taught on the Pala Indian Reservation for three years. The Pala Indian Reservation sits in the middle of San Luis Rey River Valley in northern San Diego County, California, east of the community of Fallbrook. Historic variant names used to describe the area include Mission Indian Reservation and Mission Indian Reserve. It is a 12,273-acre reservation, home to a majority of the 918 enrolled members of the Cupeño and Luiseño Indians.

Belle married William Benchley in 1906 and the couple had one son. There does not seem to be much information about William, though they were together for sixteen years. Belle and William divorced in 1922 when their son, Edward, was a teenager. This left Belle with the primary responsibility of raising and supporting their child. She returned to San Diego and took a class in bookkeeping, working part-time in the County Assessor's office. Belle was the first woman ever to serve on the Board of Education in Fullerton, California. She served two consecutive terms.

In 1925, Dr. Harry M. Wegeforth, President of the Zoological Society and founder of the San Diego Zoo, offered Belle the position of temporary bookkeeper at the Zoological Gardens. This position seemed a natural fit for Belle. She was excited and accepted the offer. On her first day, after being on the job for a scant hour, she received a strange phone call. It seems a man wanted to settle a bet with a friend, and he asked, "How long is a hippopotamus' tail?" It was at this point Belle realized her job was going to encompass much more than bookkeeping. This proved to be true!

This was just the first of many calls challenging Belle's curiosity and sending her in search of information and answers. Her duties included the care and feeding of between 600 and 800 animals, housed on 150-acres, collecting the ten cents requisite admission fee from visitors, and soliciting for both payroll funds and food for the animals. Belle also lectured widely about the zoo, making for some endless days. When asked later in her life what a day in her life looked like, her reply was perfect and honest: "whatever the day brings forth," and so it was for many years.

In October 1927, Belle was promoted to a top position as the zoo's executive secretary. A common belief of the day was that women were well-suited for secretarial work. It was one of only a few "acceptable" careers for a woman. Belle began taking her lunch breaks out in the zoo, visiting all the animals. When she found problems, she reported them to Dr. Wegeforth. When he could, he acted, but he needed a Zoo Director. He chose four men as potential directors, who showed great promise, but on closer examination and a subsequent interview, he found them woefully lacking. Weary and at his wit's end, Dr. Wegeforth offered the job to Belle, saying, "go ahead and run the place, you're doing it, anyway." Insightful man.

Belle accepted, and it's where she stayed until her retirement in 1953. She was, for most of her career, the only woman Zoo Director in the world. Owing to her leadership as director, annual attendance increased more than fourfold, and the budget increased more than sevenfold. What an exciting time this must have been for Belle. It was much more than just a job for her.

It would be remiss not to mention a little about the extraordinary man who was Harry Milton Wegeforth. As a child, he exhibited a great love of animals, reading many animal behavior books. He always had a particular love of turtles and tortoises. When he was twelve, he spent time at a local big top while performers practiced. He became quite adept on the tightrope, and they invited him to go on tour! His older brother convinced him that was not the best life choice. Harry was quite remarkable in many other ways as well. He earned a medical degree from the University of Maryland and did postgraduate work at Johns Hopkins University, where he specialized in surgery. Harry had a thriving medical practice in San Diego and served briefly as president of the City Board of Health and as a surgeon for the San Diego and Arizona Railway. He also established a hospital and clinic in the city's downtown district. Harry always had a deep love and respect for animals and when he saw animals being exploited in small cages along Park Boulevard in downtown San Diego, in what he called "little more than Menagerie Row," he acted. Using largely personal funds at first, he acquired land and built the San Diego Zoo, and established the Zoological Society of San Diego. Yet Harry was always very self-effacing and humble, most often crediting others for his work.

In her first few weeks on the job as the new director, Belle performed all the various tasks of her 125 employees to better understand the daily operations of the zoo. She cleaned elephant cages, nursed a sick emu, and patrolled the grounds as the night watchman.

Belle believed the zoo was for the animals, not for the people. In the early days, there was some resentment that she was a woman in that position, and she took a little flack, but Belle proved her worth and was soon called "The Zoo Lady." When *TIME* magazine interviewed her in 1930, she told the reporter: "They spoiled the world's best cook to make a Zoo Director out of me. I do not see why more women do not go in for it."

Elephants had been at the zoo since its opening, but the first large donation was a bear that had been a pet on a Navy ship. This beloved pet had grown too big and active to keep on board, so when the ship pulled into port, "Caesar" was donated to the zoo. Newly established and struggling financially, the zoo had no way of transporting her. So, they "made do", as was often the case. They placed a collar around Caesar's neck and attached a chain "leash." Caesar rode regally in the front seat of a passenger car to her new home. What an amazing sight that must have been.

Over the years, sailors often donated their pet bears as they grew too big for the ships, keeping the zoo well stocked. Just why the Navy kept gaining bears as pets is a mystery, but that is probably a story for another time.

In Belle's first year as director, she instituted the school bus program. The zoo had two buses used to transport children to and from the zoo. Belle provided an educational tour and introduced the children to each of the residents. In 1985, that program was still running, enriching the lives of over

150,000 children. The program continues in an expanded form today.

Belle and Dr. Wegeforth were a dynamic team, functioning like a well-oiled machine. She called him "Dr. Harry" and he called her "girl" or as the years went on, "old girl." Together, they oversaw the zoo as it grew, increased the number and species of animals, and developed a very innovative design plan.

This design plan, the first of its nature, focused on a more natural environment for the animals by creating "cageless" exhibits. The climate in San Diego was perfect for such a design. This plan reinforced Belle's belief that zoos were for animals and recognized that animals kept in small, sparse cages, were subject to the whims of spectators who were sometimes very cruel. Not surprisingly, animals cease to thrive in small, confined spaces and most often become depressed. Belle and Harry recognized this and knew that species could live for decades in the wild, but in contrast, often died within a year under the cramped conditions of classical zoos. In the United States, the record for keeping koala bears alive was four days.

The popular belief was that zoos were there to make money by displaying animals to people. The audience was the first concern. The health, comfort, and safety of the animals were secondary if a concern at all. Belle and Harry believed the animals must come first and worked tirelessly to ensure this.

Belle had an extraordinary devotion to all these animals and a second sense of sorts for their health. Often, she would detect an illness before keepers or veterinarians noticed it. Her observation would be that the animal "just didn't look quite right." Her talent in this area was legendary. Belle became widely known as an expert in animal behavior and zoo strategies. This notoriety extended around the globe.

Belle was the first female president of the American Zoological Association and a member of the International Union of Directors of Zoological Gardens. After thirteen years on the job, Belle published her book, *My Life in a Manmade Jungle.* In it, she confessed she was the director but also a housekeeper, consulting physician, dietitian, and homemaker to an enormous family of adopted animals. Belle learned the individual likes, dislikes, eccentricities, and personalities of each animal. She soon realized they were quite complex, temperamental, and every bit as unique as humans.

Belle's deep respect and care extended to all the animals living at the zoo. She would tolerate no abuse or neglect, warning her employees to always use "a soft word instead of a club, a gentle twinkle of the eye instead of a whip." She demanded and received the utmost care for all her charges.

Each day, Belle took a drive through the entire zoo to monitor things. She fiercely championed the concept of a natural environment to protect her charges as they lived and bred. She insisted they must live in the best possible way, not stressed by confinement. They must live in a natural and comfortable setting. To assure this was accomplished, scientists were consulted during the design of these living spaces. The animals were to be given adequate space, with terrain features that matched the animals' original habitat, and a diet as close to their natural diet as possible. Belle was the first to use moats as a natural barrier for bears and big cats. She made sure each area had a private place out of public view as a retreat. She had wolves moved to larger spaces and wrote articles for the paper explaining their ideologies and promoting the zoo.

Some criticized Belle for supporting the removal of animals from their natural habitat. Many still offer that criticism today, and maybe rightly so, despite the radical changes made in zoos across the country. However, Belle was doing her job the best way she knew how. She believed the environment she was planning and creating would yield the very best life for animals in any zoo setting.

In 1931, Belle acquired, at no small expense, two gorillas, Mbongo and Ngagi, (the largest in captivity). This put the San Diego Zoo in the limelight since there were only five in the country. Born in the Belgian Congo, they were first thought to be mountain gorillas, but upon capture, it was discovered they were lowland gorillas. When they arrived at the zoo, they were five years old. The plan was they would be observed, studied, and hopefully, they would breed, but it was soon noted that they were both males. So much for the breeding aspect of the acquisition!

Belle fell in love with those gorillas, stopping by each day to offer them treats. She became like a grandmother to Mbongo and Ngagi, garnering a lot of positive publicity for the zoo. She said that Mbongo, at 600-plus pounds, was "friendly, comical, and apt to be a little tricky." Of Ngagi she said, "there are few people Ngagi even tolerates, and he shows his resentment of photographers, or too close observance, especially when eating." Ngagi did love Belle, and showed her great affection, often lying down next to the fence so she could scratch his head. In her book, *My Friends, the Apes*, she wrote about him.

When Mbongo died in 1942, Belle was disconsolate, mourning his loss. She said, "Never has the death of any animal in the San Diego Zoo created so much personal feeling of sorrow or regret as that of Mbongo." There are bronze busts of these two gentle giants at the zoo today, and it is said that they are often the most photographed subjects.

Belle opened the largest bird enclosure in the world for birds of prey, complete with hills, cliffs, and trees. She was also quite proud of the zoo hospital, with a sophisticated and innovative nursery, the first in the United States. She was equally proud of the highly successful captive breeding program.

The zoo family continued to grow, housing very popular attractions. Giraffes, known as Lofty and Peaches, became residents in 1938. Five years later, Loftus was the first hippo born at the zoo. Then came Diablo, the twenty-three-foot python, who was also a big attention-getter. Two snow leopards, believed to be the first in captivity, joined the zoo in 1949. That same month, it snowed in the city for the first time in a century. Some did not believe it was a coincidence.

Belle gained further notoriety through her public speaking engagements, delivering around 150 lectures. She also used radio and newsreels and contributed articles to various magazines. Belle authored a memoir, *My Animal Babies,* and a children's book *Shirley Visits the Zoo.*

The books Belle had published were lively and anecdotal, bringing more public attention to the zoo. She served as a role model and mentor to her junior staff members, many of whom stayed on at the zoo, rising to administrative positions. During the war, when the male population was reduced, she hired several women as keepers.

Belle retired on December 10, 1953. The San Diego Zoo marked the day as "Belle Benchley Day." Over 800 people attended a farewell dinner. Belle received countless tributes and a trip around the world. In 1963 she returned to the zoo for the Belle Benchley Plaza dedication.

On September 5, 1969, the mayor of San Diego presented Belle with a citation and an Outstanding Citizen Award that celebrated her as the first woman in the world to manage a zoo and for making their zoo "the greatest in the world."

The San Diego Zoo today is the pride of the region, running extensive programs for the education and preservation of endangered species, and the storage of genetic information of extinct species, while continuing to push the boundaries of natural enclosures pioneered by Belle and Dr. Harry a century ago. Every zoo today, in some way and to some degree, is an echo of the Benchley Model.

The author Margery Facklam included Belle Benchley in her book *Wild Animals Gentle Women*, featuring eleven influential women such as Jane Goodall and Dian Fossey.

In 2007, Belle was inducted into the San Diego Women's Hall of Fame.

Suggestions for further reading:

The Zoo Lady: Belle Benchley and the San Diego Zoo by Margaret Poynter

It Began with a Roar! The story of the World-Famous San Diego Zoo by Harry M. Wegeforth and Neil Morgan

Elizabeth "Bessie" Coleman

Photo Credit: Getty Images

"I refused to take no for an answer"

Elizabeth "Bessie" Coleman was born in Atlanta, Texas, on January 26, 1892, in a one-room cabin with a dirt floor. Bessie was the tenth of thirteen children. Her father, George Coleman, was Cherokee and African American, and her mother, Susan, was African American. They were loving parents and hard-working sharecroppers.

Bessie's family moved to Waxahachie, Texas, when she was two. When she turned six, Bessie began school in a one-room, segregated schoolhouse, walking four miles a day to attend. She was bright and loved school, especially reading, which was her favorite subject, though she also excelled in math. Bessie graduated after completing all eight grades, which was highly unusual for the times.

Each year, Bessie's education was interrupted by the cotton harvest and caring for her younger siblings, though she still achieved the highest grades in her class. Bessie's mother, although illiterate herself, recognized her daughter's intelligence and drive. She made certain all her children made good use of the traveling library that came through town several times a year. Bessie was always proud of who she was, and of her race. This was something she learned from her hardworking and devout mother.

After she finished her schoolwork, Bessie would read to her mother and siblings, establishing herself as a pillar of the Coleman family at a very young age.

Bessie said the one book that influenced and inspired her the most was Frank Baum's *The Wonderful Wizard of Oz*, written in 1900. It is the chronicle of a scared little girl forced into a cruel world. She meets three strangers who, like her, feel they are incomplete. They join forces to seek "Oz" who is reported to be able to fix everyone and everything. In the process, the four discover they already have everything they thought was missing, right inside themselves. This spoke to Bessie.

In 1901, having a difficult time supporting his family, and because being Indian in Texas in those days was even more dangerous than being "Colored," Bessie's father, George, left Texas. He returned to Oklahoma, or Indian Territory as it was known then, to look for better opportunities. He had relatives there and some land rights. Susan, with five small children still at home, refused to go with him. She remained behind and supported the children by picking cotton and taking in laundry and ironing. As the children grew, they helped with these tasks as well.

When Bessie was twelve, she was accepted into the Missionary Baptist School on a scholarship. She saved any money she could earn. After graduation, she took her savings and enrolled in the Oklahoma Colored Agricultural and Normal University (since renamed Langston University) in Langston, Oklahoma. She completed one term before her meager savings ran out. Unfortunately, Bessie had to leave school and return home, where she worked as a laundress.

In 1915, when Bessie was twenty-three years old, she moved to Chicago. Two of her brothers were already established there, so she went to live with them. She attended Burnham School of Beauty Culture, taking a course in manicuring. Bessie was always determined to "better" herself, and though it seems she still did not have a clear idea of what that would look like, she kept moving forward. She found work as a manicurist at the White Sox Barber Shop, then owned by the trainer of Chicago's American League baseball club. Here, Bessie heard many stories about pilots returning home from the war, and their adventures in flying. She voraciously read all the stories of World War I pilots she could get her hands on. Her brothers fueled the flames of her desire to fly, telling stories of French women who flew during the war. Bessie devoured these stories and realized that she had an acute passion for aviation. This might just be her path.

What was believed to be the single worst incident of racial violence in America occurred in Chicago, during of summer of 1919. A Black youth on a homemade raft mistakenly drifted into an area of Lake Michigan that was a "whites-only" area. The whites stoned him, and he fell into the water and drowned. That very night, Chicago erupted into total chaos and violence, with whites and Blacks fighting in the streets with knives and guns and setting fires. When dawn came, a gang of angry whites attacked a streetcar, dragging Blacks off and beating them to death. It took the National Guard four days to restore order in the city. Fortunately, Bessie and her brothers were not attacked, but there were thirty-eight dead, 537 injured, and over 1,000 homeless. It was a complete disaster, with death and destruction everywhere.

Bessie must have felt like Dorothy in *The Wonderful Wizard of Oz.* She had traveled that "yellow brick road," and that road that was chock full of conflict and difficulties. But she held fast to her dreams and was unwavering in her quest to succeed. She fought long and hard against the evils of racism, sexism, poverty, and ignorance.

When Bessie's brother John teasingly said to her one day, "you nigger women ain't never goin' to fly. Not like those women I saw in France." It hit the mark. He announced this in public, at the barbershop. It was a moment of awakening for her. Bessie remained calm, smiled, and looked him in the eye, saying, "That's it - you just called it for me." That was when it all cemented in her brain and strengthened her will even more. She would fly!

Bessie soon discovered, however, that American Aviation Schools refused to admit women or Blacks to train as pilots. She was both, and she was proud of it! Bessie would not be deterred. She had made up her mind. There was no turning back for her. She had made the acquaintance of Robert S. Abbott, who was the founder and publisher of the *Chicago Defender*. Abbott recognized and admired Bessie's dedication and passion. He encouraged her to study abroad. She received financial backing from his paper, as well as from a local banker, Jesse Binga, who also recognized something special about this determined young woman. Bessie was on her way.

Still saving her earnings, and more determined than ever, Bessie took a French language class at the Berlitz school in Chicago, eventually making her way to Paris on November 29, 1920, to earn her pilot's license. Her instruction was on a Nieuport 82 biplane with a "steering system that consisted of a vertical stick in the thickness of a baseball bat in front of the pilot and a rudder bar under the pilot's feet."

On June 15, 1921, Bessie Coleman became the first woman of African American and Native American descent to earn an aviation pilot's license. France's most famous flight school issued it - Ecole d'Aviation des Frères Caudron et Le Crotoy - managed by French aviators and plane designers Gaston and Rene' Caudron. She was also the first person of

African American and Native American descent to earn an international aviation license from the Federation Aeronautique Internationale, #18.310.

Bessie continued to polish her skills and spent the next two months taking intensive lessons from a French ace pilot near Paris. While in Europe, Bessie attended the Second Pan-African Congress Paris Session spearheaded by William Edward Burghardt DuBois. (WEB DuBois was one of the eminent African American scholars of the time and was an American sociologist, socialist, historian, civil rights activist, Pan-Africanist, author, writer, and editor). He spoke and wrote that his intent was to "emerge with a program of Pan-Africanism, as organized protection of the Negro world led by American Negroes." He espoused a desire, and of course, Bessie did as well, to use aviation as a means of upward mobility for the "Race." Bessie must have felt as if he was speaking directly to her.

In September 1921, Bessie sailed to New York. When she entered the United States, she was an instant media sensation. Well, the Black press celebrated her, but the mainstream white press largely ignored her.

In Tulsa, Oklahoma, history once again was made. The June 1, 1921, race riot greatly affected and shaped African Americans' perceptions of aviation. The reason? After an unresolved lynching, six white pilots dropped bombs on the Greenwood district of Tulsa, setting fire to the town, and killing hundreds of residents. It was called the "Black Wall Street," because of the concentration of prominent African American professionals and businesses. They razed the neighborhood within hours. This violent event is alarmingly absent from most, if not all, mainstream history books.

This marked the first time in U.S. history that airplanes were used to attack an American community, and this community was Black. Tempers flared and outrage was expressed. Marcus Garvey spoke and encouraged African Americans to become aviators, securing as many airplanes as possible in anticipation of a violent race war. Garvey was a Jamaican political activist, publisher, journalist, entrepreneur, and orator. He was the founder and first President of the Universal Negro Improvement Association and the African Communities League. The Black press promoted aviation to dispel the rampant stereotypes that portrayed African Americans as less intelligent, incompetent, and lazy. Bessie Coleman was now doing what everyone was talking about.

A true highlight of Bessie's career was receiving a silver loving cup from the cast of the current Broadway show, "Shuffle Along," which was a musical tribute to her achievements. The cup was a gesture of respect and admiration, but also one of recognition of the odds that she had defied. The show was a work of acknowledgment and respect. It premiered on Broadway in 1921 with music and lyrics written by Noble Sissle and Eubie Blake. It became such a hit, and so popular, that it caused huge traffic jams in the city. It was also the show that launched the careers of Josephine Baker and Paul Robeson. Bessie gave the cup to her mother and told the press that she would perform exhibition flights to inspire other African Americans to fly.

Back in New York, Bessie publicly outlined her goals for the rest of her life. She would be a leader and introduce aviation to her race and gender. She would establish a school that would accept and encourage anyone with a dream of flying. She would speak in schools, churches, and theaters to highlight and spark the interest of fellow African and Native Americans in this new and ever-expanding technology of flight. Bessie was intelligent, well-spoken, and beautiful. She often embellished stories and exaggerated her already amazing accomplishments to get bigger audiences and better publicity. As a result, the press dubbed her "Queen Bess."

Bessie was now ready to seek employment. She also wanted to purchase an airplane with which she could demonstrate her skill. However, now that she was back in America, she was stonewalled in her bids to purchase a plane or gain work in commercial aviation. Once again, she was crushed by the treatment she received in America, but she did not give up. Remember, this was Bessie Coleman! She would not take "no" for an answer. It just wasn't in her.

Bessie soon realized that to make a living as a civilian in America, and with the age of commercial flight still a decade away, she would have to become a stunt flier, a barnstormer, playing to the public and audiences everywhere she could. She would need more training and a lot of practice. No one in Chicago, or anywhere nearby, was willing to teach her. She would have to go back to Europe.

In May 1922, she crossed the Atlantic again. Her goal was to get hands-on advanced training and more experience in aviation back in France, Germany, Holland, and Switzerland. She studied with the famous WWI German ace fighter pilot, Captain Keller. She tested a few airplanes in the Netherlands for Anthony Fokker, dubbed the Flying Dutchman. Fokker was a Dutch aviation pioneer, aviation entrepreneur, aircraft designer, and aircraft manufacturer. He produced fighter aircraft in Germany during the First World War, such as the Eindecker monoplane, the Dr. I triplane (simply known as the Fokker Triplane), and the Fokker D. VII biplane, and designed one of the most popular fighter planes used during the war.

These professionals not only recognized Bessie's skill, but they also trusted her, treating her as an equal, which she certainly was at this point. She practiced, day in and day out; figure eights, loop-the-loops, trick climbs, landing the airplane with the engine cut, perfecting high flying, refining safety maneuvers, and turning them all into polished acrobatic stunts. Bessie was celebrated in Germany for flying the largest and most awkward plane ever flown by a woman, the Boeing B-29 Superfortress. After a few months of intensive training, she returned to the United States with the skill and confidence necessary to launch her career in exhibition flying. She became a media sensation, admired by many this time.

On September 3, 1922, Bessie took part in her first air show at Curtis Airfield in Garden City, a small village in Long Island, New York. It was Labor Day, and she put together a show that would appeal to the public and their patriotism while honoring African American equality. Perhaps she had been inspired by the words of W.E.B. Du Bois, who sought to "make it possible for a man to be both a Negro and American without being cursed and spit upon by his fellows…"

Bessie dedicated the show to the 15th Regiment of Infantry, which was the first African American regiment to be sent to France during WWI. The Glenn Curtiss Airplane Company provided the plane for the event. Curtiss Aeroplane and Motor Company was an American aircraft manufacturer formed in 1916 by Glenn Hammond Curtiss. After significant commercial success in the early part of the century, it merged with Wright Aeronautical in 1929 to form Curtiss-Wright Aviation Corporation. The crowd was large, the temperatures mild, and the skies were clear. It was a perfect day, and it ended with the offering of individual rides in Bessie's plane at the cost of $5 per person, which today would equate to about $60.

The thrill of stunt flying, and the cheering of admiring crowds, was just a part of Bessie's dream. She never forgot her childhood vow to one day "amount to something." Despite her flamboyant style, or maybe because of it, she was gaining a reputation as a skilled and daring pilot, who stopped at nothing to execute a difficult stunt.

Bessie flew the Curtiss JN-4 "Jenny" which was a biplane and an army surplus aircraft left over from the war. In 1923 she bought a small plane but crashed it on the way to her first scheduled West Coast air show. This time, the story needed no embellishment, but it didn't dampen her enthusiasm. The plane was a total loss, and Bessie required hospitalization for several months. She suffered a broken leg, broken ribs, and other injuries. But she was made of tough stuff, and sent a message to her adoring public, "Tell them all that as soon as I can walk, I'm going to fly!"

Bessie returned to Chicago to recover from her injuries, which were extensive. While she completed her recovery, she was soliciting funds and backers to continue her work. It took her eighteen months to obtain enough capital for a series of shows in Texas.

The summer of 1925 brought Bessie outstanding success, and she earned enough to put a down payment on another plane. Her body may have been injured, but her spirit was unbroken. Bessie Coleman was becoming well known, and this fame brought her steady work. She felt that her dream of opening a school for aviators was now within her reach and close to becoming a reality. It was an exciting time for her, as her tenacity and hard work were paying off.

Bessie was offered a role in a feature-length film that was titled, "Shadow and Sunshine," which she accepted. It flattered her. The African American Seminole Film Production Company financed it. She hoped that the publicity and any royalties would help in advancing her career and provide some capital to establish the flying school she envisioned, which was so important to her. She always had her eye on the prize.

The glitch came in the first scene when the director required Bessie to appear in ragged and tattered clothes, using a walking stick and a backpack on her back. She immediately refused, turned, and walked away without looking back, when she realized that the depiction of her as a Black woman would be a stereotypical "Uncle Tom." For Bessie, it was a statement of principle, which meant more to her than fame or money. Those of her backers, who were in the entertainment industry, walked away from supporting her career. Bessie may have been daring, and as some claimed, even opportunistic about her career, but she was never an opportunist about race. Bessie had absolutely no intention of ever perpetuating the derogatory image that many whites held of Blacks. Remember, Bessie was proud of who she was in all regards, including her race. It was a financial blow, but her sense of self and her worth remained intact.

Bessie's career had taken off. She was flying and made regular appearances at air shows. She was mostly living her dream and moving toward establishing her flight school. On April 30, 1926, Bessie purchased a plane in Dallas, Texas, and had it sent to Florida for a big airshow. Her friends and family were concerned about the safety of the plane and begged her not to fly it yet. It needed a thorough check before she would fly it. She had the crew, led by her mechanic, William Wills, who was also her publicity agent, go over the plane from one end to the other. They deemed it flight worthy and gave her the thumbs up. She trusted it would be fine.

They took off for a test flight with Wills piloting and Bessie in the other seat. Bessie had her seatbelt unbuckled so she could lean out and get a better view of the ground as she planned the next day's stunts. Among other things, a parachute jump was planned. They were ten minutes into the flight when the plane did not pull out of an intended nosedive. It gained speed and went into a wild tailspin. Bessie was thrown from the plane, from about five hundred feet, and died upon impact. Despite valiant efforts, Wills could not gain control of the plane and it crashed. He also died on impact, and the plane burst into flames. It was an extremely sad and tragic day.

The wreckage of the plane was badly charred, but in reconstructing the accident, they discovered a wrench, used to service the engine earlier that day, had slid into the gearbox and jammed it, causing the plane to spin out of control and crash, taking with it two lives.

Elizabeth "Bessie" Coleman's funeral was on May 2, 1926, in Jacksonville, Florida, and was attended by 5,000 mourners. Many members of Black society, including Ida B. Wells, were in attendance. On May

5, in Orlando, Florida, thousands more attended a funeral for her at the Mount Zion Missionary Church. Her last journey was to Chicago's Pilgrim Baptist Church, where it was estimated that 10,000 paid their respects all night and into the next day. After the final funeral services, Bessie was interred in the Lincoln Cemetery.

Bessie Coleman was gone, but over the years, recognition of her many accomplishments have only grown. She had a tremendous impact on aviation history. In 1927, Bessie Coleman Aero Clubs sprang up throughout the country.

On Labor Day in 1931, the first all-African American Air Show was sponsored, which attracted approximately 15,000 spectators. It was in that same year that a group of African American pilots began an annual flyover of Coleman's grave.

In 1989, the First Flight Society, which honors individuals that have achieved significant "firsts" in aviation's development and history, inducted Bessie into their ranks.

The Federal Aviation Administration in Washington, D.C. named a conference room after Bessie.

In 1990 Mayer Richard M. Daley renamed the Old Mannheim Road at O'Hare International Airport the "Bessie Coleman Drive." In 1992 he proclaimed May 2, as "Bessie Coleman Day in Chicago."

In 1993, Mae Jemison, who is a physician and former NASA astronaut, published a book about Bessie, *Queen Bess: Daredevil Aviator*. In it, she says, "I point to Bessie Coleman and say without hesitation that here is a woman, a being, who exemplifies and serves as a model for all humanity; the very definition of strength, dignity, courage, integrity, and beauty. It looks like a good day for flying."

In 1995, Bessie was honored with her image on a U.S. postage stamp, and she was inducted into the Woman in Aviation Hall of Fame.

In November 2000, Bessie Coleman was inducted into the Texas Aviation Hall of Fame.

Suggestions for further reading:

The Life of Bessie Coleman: First African American Woman Pilot by Connie Plantz

Queen Bess: Daredevil Aviator by Doris L. Rich, Mae Jemison

Bessie Coleman: Queen of the Skies by Phyllis J. Perry

Bessie Coleman: Trailblazing Pilot, Rookie Biographies by Carol Alexander, Jodie Shepherd

Clara Brown

Photo Credit: Colorado Historical Society

"I always go where Jesus calls me."

Clara Brown was born into slavery in Spotsylvania County, Virginia, near Fredericksburg, on January 1, 1800. Accounts differ slightly on birth dates and place. What we know for certain is that at a very young age, she, along with her mother, was sold to

Ambrose Smith, a tobacco farmer, to work in his tobacco fields. Smith was a kindly man, a devout Methodist, and took Clara and her mother with his family to church services. Life with the Smith family was tolerable for a slave.

Clara was a tall, strong woman with warm brown eyes. At age eighteen, she married Richard, also a slave, who worked as a carpenter on the Smith plantation. Masters encouraged slaves to marry and produce children to work for them. Clara and Richard had four children, Richard, Margaret, Paulina Ann, and Eliza Jane. Paulina Ann drowned when she was eight years old.

In 1835, their owner Ambrose Smith died. Part of the estate settlement was to bring the Brown family to the auction. Clara watched in abject horror as it broke apart the family. They were all sold separately to different owners. Each was sent to different and distant locations with their new owner. George Brown, a plantation owner from Logan County, Kentucky, sensed that Clara was strong and intelligent, so he placed high bids to buy her. Sold! She had a new master and did not know where the rest of her family had gone. Clara vowed that day to search for the rest of her life for her family, especially her youngest daughter, ten-year-old Eliza Jane. For twenty years Clara worked for George Brown as a housemaid; loving and raising his children rather than her own. Her heart was breaking.

When Clara was fifty-three years old, she was freed. Although Kentucky slavery was a brutal enterprise, in some ways Kentucky was more lenient in its laws than several other slave states. For example, Kentucky never passed laws that outlawed teaching slaves to read and write, never prohibited owners from freeing their slaves, and never forced freed people to leave the state. Clara, her heart aching for the family she had lost, left the state. She knew she would search until the end of her days to find her daughter.

Rumors showed that Eliza Jane had moved west a few years earlier. The rumor mill was always active. Clara immediately headed for St. Louis where she thought Missouri law protected free Blacks. In Kentucky, she didn't feel safe, as highwaymen were marauding and kidnapping free Blacks and selling them back to unscrupulous plantation owners. Easy money!

Searching for three years, beginning in Kentucky, Missouri, and Kansas, and to no avail, Clara wondered if perhaps Eliza Jane had joined the masses that had gone to Pikes Peak, hoping to find gold. The big mining boom began in July 1858 and lasted until February 1861. Maybe she should head to Colorado Territory. Clara must have felt like she was chasing a ghost.

In April 1859, Clara made the 700-mile trip west into the Colorado Territory gold fields. She had saved enough money for the trip, but Blacks could not ride stages. Fortunately, she met Colonel Benjamin Wadsworth, whose wagon train was going to Colorado. The Colonel offered Clara a job as a cook for free transportation. The journey was long, dusty, and arduous. Clara ended up walking most of the way. According to some accounts, she was the first Black woman to cross the plains during the gold rush. After a few months, with no sign of Eliza Jane,

Clara headed further west toward Denver, ending up in Auraria.

Clara started working in a bakery and as a laundress. She was very spiritual and was used to working hard. Clara's faith kept her going. She, along with two Methodist missionary ministers, founded the non-denominational Union Sunday school. (Clara saw a need as miners rushed into the mountains, by droves, to pan for precious metals). She also set up the first laundry in Gilpin County, in Gregory Gulch, later called Central City, Colorado.

Central City consisted of gold mines, stores, and saloons, as well as shacks where miners lived with their families. Clara also worked as a midwife, cook, and nursemaid in the area. This was a boom time, and her work brought Clara a substantial income. She expanded her laundry business and hired an assistant. Clara collected whatever gold dust came out of the miners' pockets and made extra money by cooking and cleaning for the miners. She worked long hours and saved most of what she made, denying herself any luxuries, and spending her money only on essentials. With these savings, she funded the construction of St. James Methodist Church. Clara assisted freed slaves in relocating to Colorado. She grubstaked miners with no other means of support while they looked for gold in the mountains. They often repaid her handsomely for her kindness and generosity when they struck pay dirt. Clara gave generously to Euro-Americans and Native Americans. Her heart knew no boundaries. Her home was a hospital, a general refuge for anyone who needed it. She often said, "I always go where Jesus calls me."

Clara was wise and when she had saved up enough money, invested in land and mining claims. Within several years, she had saved $10,000 and owned sixteen lots in Denver, seven houses in Central City, mines, and property in Boulder, Georgetown, and Idaho Springs. She was now supporting herself very well.

Clara was considered a hub in her town. Her businesses and her home were vital pieces of this community. Sick or injured miners, regardless of race or creed, would turn to Clara for help. She gave them a place to heal and recover, caring for them with great tenderness until they could return to work. She also helped the homeless who needed a place to stay. Pregnant women often asked Clara to care for them and help deliver their babies. She provided these services for free to those who could not afford them.

Clara was a fervent Presbyterian, but she never discriminated against any faith. She generously gave money and time to four different churches in town. As she had done before, she helped start the first Sunday School class, often using her home as the classroom. In addition, she provided financial help to young women attending Oberlin College. Her faith and her position in the community were strong and her finances were very secure. She was called by many, "The Angel of the Rockies" and "Aunt Clara."

However, Clara was still missing something—her family. She offered her entire fortune as a reward for any word leading to reuniting her with Eliza Jane. Sadly, she received word that her other daughter, Margaret, had died. Two of her four children were dead. She did not know where Eliza Jane was, and she had lost track of both her surviving son, Richard, and her husband years ago.

Since the Civil War had ended and travel was once again safe, she liquidated most of her remaining assets and holdings and returned to Kentucky to search again for her daughter. After an exhausting search, Clara still had not found Eliza Jane. Along the way, she encountered sixteen freed women and men, some of whom were relatives. Clara paid their way to travel with her back to Colorado, where she helped them get settled.

Unfortunately, disaster was just around the corner, even as new communities flourished. A great flood swept mercilessly through the land and destroyed much of Denver with many losing properties, including Clara. In fact, it was the first deadly flood in Denver's history. A spring rainstorm caused flash flooding along the Cherry and Plum creeks. Between fifteen and twenty people perished.

In 1873, Clara's home and several of her remaining properties went up in flames during a huge fire in Central City. Although the city council passed a referendum that they could build no new wood frame buildings in the business district, it came too late for some. The fire began in Dostal Alley behind Main Street. It destroyed about 150 buildings in the downtown area. Clara was left with nothing to show for years of hard work. As one of the most hard-working and prosperous people in the area, she was now without a home and was devastated. People in the community joined forces to help Clara, just as she had done for so many over the years. In her own time of crisis, the town lovingly returned Clara's kindness by setting her up in a comfortable, little cottage.

In 1879, Clara made a return trip to Kansas. Her goal was to assist other former slaves as they moved to Colorado to "build a community and farm the land." There were jobs available in Colorado because of mining strikes and labor shortages. She was an official representative of Colorado Governor Pitkin, who sent her to persuade some of the freed Blacks to come to Colorado and homestead. History has termed this the "Black Exodus." She delivered the governor's invitation to come to Colorado and donated some of her own money to help support the new communities.

Clara was now seventy-nine years old, and despite her continuous search, still had not found her daughter, Eliza Jane. Her heart was sore, her spirit exhausted, but she still had hope.

In 1882, after forty-seven years of searching seemingly everywhere, along with a huge letter-writing campaign to officials in various locations, Clara received news that a Black woman named Eliza Jane was living in Council Bluffs, Iowa. She looked a lot like Clara and was about the right age to be her daughter. With the help and support of friends, she immediately made travel arrangements to meet this woman. Could this really be her long-lost daughter, Eliza Jane? She was! Finally!! Not only was she reunited with her daughter, but Clara met Cindy, her granddaughter. It was a momentous occasion. The discovery of her daughter turned her lifelong dream into reality. Her time of searching was over. The newspaper in Council Bluffs published an account of this miraculous and heartwarming reunion on March 4, 1882. The reporter said that Clara was "still strong, vigorous, tall, her hair thickly streaked with gray, her face kind." Clara and Eliza Jane returned to

Denver, where they lived together until Clara's death.

In 1885, Clara Brown was elected the first African American and the first female member of the Society of Colorado Pioneers. The Society recognized and honored pioneers who came to Colorado before 1861. "The early pioneer came to a silent wilderness. He took hold of the territory 'in the raw.' He had nothing but his hands, his energy, and his courage to start a new civilization in the wilderness." Both the Governor, James B. Grant, and Denver Mayor, John L. Routt, had great praise for Clara: "(she was) … the kind old friend whose heart always responded to the cry of distress, and who, rising from the humble position of slave to the angelic type of noblewoman, won our sympathy and commanded our respect." A noblewoman indeed.

A plaque commemorating the life of Clara Brown hangs at St. James Methodist Church in Central City, stating that her home had served as the first church in Central City.

In 1930, a chair was installed in the Central City Opera House in Clara's honor.

A stained-glass portrait of Clara is on display in the Old Supreme Court Chambers of the state Capitol in 1977. Clara Brown is "one of the 100 most influential women in the history of Colorado."

Clara Brown was inducted into the Colorado Women's Hall of Fame in 1989.

In 2003, an opera was written and performed about Clara's life, called "Gabriel's Daughter." It debuted in Central City, Colorado.

Suggestions for further reading:

Clara Brown: The Rags to Riches Story of a Freed Slave by Julie McDonald

Clara Brown: African American Pioneer (Great Lives in Colorado History)

Personages Importantes De La Historia De Colorado by Suzanne Frachetti

One More Valley, One More Hill: The Story of Aunt Clara Brown (Landmark Books) by Linda Lowery and Patricia McKissack

Abigail Jane Scott Duniway

"The World is moving, and women are moving with it."

Abigail Jane Scott was born on October 22, 1834, in a log cabin on the frontier of Groveland Township, Tazewell County, in Central Illinois, just a few miles from Fort Peoria. She was the third child of Anne

Roelofson Scott and John Tucker Scott, to whom twelve children were born and nine survived. Her family called her "Jenny" in her youth, though it was a name she didn't approve of at all in adulthood. She grew up on the family farm and was able to attend school only sporadically.

In March 1852, when Abigail was seventeen, the Scott family joined the largest migration to Oregon in American history. Anne Scott was very concerned about her health, and the health of her little ones, as they thought about this long and arduous trip. She voiced her concern vehemently and repeatedly, stating that she did not want to go. John, however, was determined and his wishes prevailed, as did the wishes of most men and particularly husbands at this time. He had organized a party of thirty people and five ox-drawn wagons to make the 2,400-mile trip to Oregon by a trail that was often challenging, at best, or completely impassable. Anne's concern was not without merit.

Each child was assigned a task for the journey, and Abigail's was keeping an accurate record of life on the trail. It was a formative experience for her. She kept a journal of the migration and filled it with expressions of joy and wonder at the magnificent landscapes they traversed, as well as with heartfelt sorrow for the losses they suffered along the way. The losses were many and profound. Tragically, Anne died of cholera on the trail somewhere near Fort Laramie that June. Could it be she had experienced a premonition in her feeling so strenuously against the trip? Maybe. Little Willie, age three, the youngest of the children, died in August and was buried somewhere along the Burnt River in Oregon.

Finally, in October 1852, after seven months, the weary travelers reached their destination, French Prairie, in Oregon's Willamette Valley. They found a broad valley covered with clusters of oaks, tall fir, and grassy prairies. It looked like an untouched wilderness, but it was actually a well-managed system, the result of thousands of years of planned burning by the native inhabitants. The river itself flowed in shallow channels across a wide floodplain. It ran high in the winter, low in the summer, and full of fish all year. There they joined relatives who had preceded them and eventually settled near Lafayette, in Yamhill County.

Early in 1853, Abigail relocated to Illinois and taught in a school that she established in Cincinnati. Abigail was a natural teacher. During this time, love also blossomed when she met Benjamin Charles Duniway. He was a handsome young rancher, prospector, and horseman. On August 1, of that same year, they married. Abigail said that he was "a sober and provident husband." The couple had six children, Clara Belle (1854), Willis Scott (1856), Hubert (1859), Wilkie Collins (1861), Clyde Augustus (1866), and Ralph Roelofson (1869). Together they worked their "backwoods" farm.

It was not long before Abigail began to resent her life of drudgery. The memory of her mother's hardships and sorrows seemed to live in her and through her. She later wrote of her life on her husband's farm in the forest: "It was work for which I was poorly fitted, chiefly because my faithful mother had worn both me and herself to a frazzle with such drudgery before I was born."

The family remained in Clackamas County and farmed until 1857 when they moved to another farm near Lafayette, which Abigail named Sunny Hillside. In her own words, "The making of new farms in the brush and timber in a pioneer community, away from civilization, though hard upon the men in building cabins, fences, barns, and bridges, is doubly trying for the women folks who, with babes in arms, are never able to mobilize as men do at their hog killings, log rolling, political gatherings, barn raisings, bridge building, etc., but must remain in solitude, a prey to their own thoughts, their chief diversion, aside from the blessed companionship of their many little ones, being the extra labor that devolves upon them to provide the meals for the men's frolics and labors that bring them together for the purposes just specified." Abigail further noted that a farm woman's chores very often included nursing and taking care of sick family members and neighbors, where, she noted, "the women did most of the work and a physician, almost always male, pocketed a generous payment."

As a young mother and wife, "Jenny Glenn" as she called herself, began writing for *The Argus,* and the *Oregon Farmer*. She frequently wrote articles for the *Salem Statesman*. Oddly enough, however, at this point in her young life, she disapproved of equal suffrage, and a woman's right to vote, and was not shy about saying so, "Women in some places are claiming rights they should not have."

Interesting that Abigail saw and wrote about the hardships the married women endured due to their inferior position, yet she still advised, "Ardent ladies may wish to control affairs of church or state, but what I want to see ladies' content...to use cradles for ballot boxes in which they have the right to plant, not votes, but voters." Abigail had a voice, and she was not shy about using it. It was very interesting to watch Abigail's life unfold and notice her changing views as she gained insight and wisdom.

In 1862, the family farm was lost because a friend, for whom Benjamin had co-signed a note, defaulted on the loan. Abigail had not been consulted about that loan, nor had she even been informed of her husband's assumption of such an obligation. It was a shocking and tragic discovery. She bitterly resented the law that allowed a family to lose their home, security, and livelihood because a man had pledged his farm as security without even consulting his wife. She felt it grossly unfair and bordering on immoral. Indeed, many might agree that it was both!

This dire situation was further compounded when Benjamin was permanently disabled shortly after in an accident that involved a runaway team of horses. Abigail had to assume full responsibility for the welfare of the family. She returned to teaching, opening, and running a small school near Lafayette. In 1866, they moved to Albany, where Abigail taught in a private school for about a year.

Abigail then opened a small millinery and notions shop, which she ran for five years. She became more and more agitated and resentful over women's unfair and unjust legal limitations. Women who came to her store often confided in her about injustice, intense hardship, mistreatment, and even violence in their homes. She objected to the moral double standard, early marriages of young girls, and debilitating 'excessive maternity.' Married women had absolutely no legal existence apart from their husbands. They could not sign contracts. They had no title to any money that they themselves may have earned, no right to property, or any claim to their children in the event of separation or divorce.

With each passing year, Abigail became a more avid supporter of women's rights. The tide had turned as she experienced some of life's injustices. Abigail kept a record of all these conversations, never using names, but she used her notes to create characters in her novels. It was during this time, while she was raising her six children, running the store, and planning her work in suffrage, that she wrote her first novel, *Captain Gray's Company* (aka *Crossing the Plains and Living in Oregon*. It was, of course, based on the diary that she had dutifully and diligently kept during their trip west. Her novel was well-received and gave her a fair amount of notoriety.

During the next few years, Abigail traveled and lectured on the issue of women's suffrage, with not only her husband's support but his encouragement. She even lobbied the state legislature occasionally. Abigail was a powerful and formidable figure, at a mere five foot six inches, stocky and possessing a wondrously deep and clear contralto voice. Her lectures took her to northern California and other states across the country, including Illinois, Iowa, Wyoming, Utah, Michigan, Minnesota, and Ohio.

In 1871, she closed her millinery shop, and the family moved to Portland. The U.S. Customs Service hired Benjamin, who had recovered sufficiently to take a job that was not strenuous. Abigail began to publish a weekly paper, *The New Northwest*. The first issue was printed on May 5, 1871. It became their family enterprise, with Ben assisting in business matters and their older sons helping with printing. The paper was devoted to women's rights and suffrage. Fully committed to her signature line, "Yours for Liberty," and guided by the paper's motto of "Free Speech, Free Press, Free People," Abigail Scott Duniway exposed and fought what she identified as social injustices. She discussed questions as diverse as the legal status of women, the treatment of the Chinese, policies related to American Indians, and the limits of Temperance and Prohibition. Her experiences both in business and life, along with listening to and recording the stories women told her at the shop, convinced her more than ever of the importance of equality. *The New Northwest* flourished for over sixteen years.

In 1886, Abigail reminisced that she regularly walked five miles every day of the year (except on Sunday) to collect subscriptions to her paper and wrote 100 pages of manuscript each week. To say she was passionate about all of this is an understatement! Before long, Abigail began lecturing throughout the Northwest as an educator and advocate of suffrage. She earned a reputation as an eloquent and dynamic speaker.

Abigail established a partnership with Susan B. Anthony, who traveled with her on a 2,400-mile lecture circuit that lasted for two months. The trip was a success in building support for suffrage, but it was also extremely physically challenging. The pair traveled "by jouncing coaches or dirty, crawling trains" often in rainy weather. Abigail wrote in her journal: "the winter rains were deluging the earth. The stage carrying us from Olympia to the Columbia River at Kalama led us through the blackness of darkness in the nighttime, giving Miss Anthony a taste of pioneering under difficulties that remained with her as a memory to her dying day."

Benjamin Duniway passed away in 1896. A saddened Abigail wrote that not only had he been a best friend, devoted husband, and father, but he had always supported the work for equal suffrage and her part in it.

Abigail encountered many setbacks, such as financial strain and insufficiency, poor health, and opposition from her brother, Harvey W. Scott, somewhat of a rival, who edited the *Oregonian*, a popular Portland newspaper. He believed that women didn't want, and should not have, the right to vote. He wrote many harsh and forceful articles on the subject. Unlike her brother Harvey, who graduated from Pacific University, Abigail was mainly self-taught and had less than a year of formal schooling back in rural Illinois. Still, she was determined to make her paper a voice for human rights, particularly suffrage, and she did. Despite the many and varied challenges, she persisted.

Abigail published a volume of poems, *My Musings*, and a long poem entitled *David and Anna Matson*. Eventually, Abigail closed her paper and became editor of a weekly paper, *Pacific Empire,* where she continued her advocacy for women and the suffrage movement. The paper included her serialized novels as a regular feature. When Leopold Samuel, editor of the *West Shore,* which was the first illustrated publication west of the Rockies, retired, Abigail, joined the staff. Again, using her writing skill as a vehicle to advance the cause of women, Abigail took up writing a regular column for this paper.

While Abigail was away in Washington DC, attending the National American Woman Suffrage Association convention, she sent regular "racy" letters back that were published in the paper. The following announcement appeared: "Mrs. A. S. Duniway will conduct a department in which the cause of womankind, politically, socially, and morally, will be a prominent feature. . . Her work will be a regular feature of the paper, and so conducted as to be fair but vigorous always. The *West Shore* offers this as one of the elements which make a public journal influential. This department is made possible by the addition of four pages to the size of the paper, and we are confident that the work will add to the interest of the paper among the people at large."

When Abigail was out lecturing, she sent editorial correspondence home for publication. It was a combination of biting commentary and travelog. She often appeared in the columns of other suffrage and women's publications including Susan B. Anthony, Elizabeth Cady Stanton, and Parker Pillsbury's "Revolution," Lucy Stone and Henry Blackwell's

"Woman's Journal," and Clara Berwick Colby's "Woman's Tribune." Clearly, she understood the power of the written and spoken word and employed both with great skill to further her cause.

Abigail also loved a good debate and truly enjoyed subtly turning the tables during the discourse. For example, in reply to the charge that equal rights would cause women to abandon home and family, she conceded women's maternal instinct and domestic inclination, arguing that these were so powerful that equal rights could not entice women to abandon them: "We have no fear of becoming the determined enemy of man. We do not believe that woman can educate herself out of herself, that she can lose her femininity by intellectual or business pursuits or eradicate the emotional side of her nature." Once, when asked whether she would be willing to join the armed forces if allowed to vote, Abigail noted that the questioner was no longer a soldier and had never been a sailor, retorting: "Then, sir, since, by your theory, nobody ought to vote unless they fight, and you are not now a fighter, ought you not to be disenfranchised along with the women?" The advancement of women's rights was for her a natural, ineluctable part of human socio-political development. "The world is moving," she was fond of saying, "and women are moving with it."

Abigail founded and presided over the Oregon Equal Suffrage Association. She was the honorary president of the Oregon Federation of Women's Clubs and was elected president of the Portland Woman's Club. She also began lobbying and was a constant presence in the Oregon State Legislature.

Abigail was quite a trailblazer but did not recognize success in her own state of Oregon. She was criticized, attacked verbally, and even subjected to physical violence for her position. This was the same year that her only daughter Clara, at age thirty-one, died of tuberculosis with Abigail at her bedside. It was a sad year for her.

Abigail was always puzzled by the consistent failure of women's suffrage referendums on her state ballots. This caused a temporary split between her and the national suffrage movement, who believed stronger management was necessary for the local branch. As a result, Abigail resigned from her position in Oregon and the national group took over.

It has been noted by several sources that she could be a bit of a difficult character, and lacked good organizational skills, but was a great crusader for the cause.

Abigail definitely had a capacity for vituperation, and it was evident in her newspaper columns and letters where she frequently engaged in name-calling, witty sarcasm, and bitter vitriol that was really very characteristic of the style of journalism of the day. Abigail lambasted Supreme Court Justice Ward Hunt, full force when he rejected the Fourteenth Amendment defense in an illegal voting trial in 1873. She called him "an angular-brained, old fossil, who would excel as a first-class donkey!" When Horace Greeley refused to endorse suffrage, she called him "an infinitesimal political pigmy of reality…a coarse, bigoted, narrow-minded old dotard." Strong words!

Abigail exchanged fire often with opposition editors, and there were many. She nicknamed one prohibition paper the "Temperance Turkey Buzzard" and denounced its editor as a "noisy simpleton." Abigail Scott Duniway could most assuredly hold her own. Later, when the State of Oregon finally acquiesced, and women gained the vote, Abigail's work was at last fully recognized and acknowledged.

In 1912, Oregon became the seventh state in the U.S. to pass a women's suffrage amendment. By now, health issues had once again begun to plague Abigail and she needed to use a wheelchair. She was asked by the Governor, Oswald West, to write the Equal Suffrage Proclamation and she was the first female to register to vote in Multnomah County, and the first female to vote in Oregon. Abigail was also the first woman summoned for jury duty.

Abigail and her newspaper strenuously supported the Sole Tender Bill and the Married Women's Property Act which, when passed, finally gave Oregon women the right to own, manage and control property. In her words: "Similarly, equal suffrage will lead to financial independence and stability for both sexes because women's improved status will call forth a heightened moral sense in men: When women become voters … they will have taken the first step to becoming lawmakers. And when they are lawmakers, their equality in property rights will follow as a natural sequence. Then … men will delight in reforming themselves voluntarily, that they may be considered worthy of the love and honor that free, enlightened, independent womanhood can alone bestow."

Abigail was never one to mince words! She was brilliant in her diplomacy and made sure to lavish praise on the brave men of the Pacific Northwest, in particular those who cleared and settled the land. No easy task! She focused on their hard work, love of liberty, and their sense of decency and fairness. In a similar way, she praised the pioneer women of the region. After all, Abigail had been one and still was! She talked about their undying strength, courage, and endurance; the great hardships they faced that were at least as great as those faced by men; their childbearing and rearing, domestic toil, and their other accomplishments in business and professions.

In 1902 in "A Pioneer Incident" Abigail wrote, "men and women who first take up their line of march across untracked continents, who settle upon the outposts of civilization and raise the standard of Liberty for all the people to higher planes are the very best and most enterprising citizens of any land." Praise of women's exploits demonstrated that women had *EARNED* equal rights. Abigail's most explicit writing on this theme is found in *Success in Sight* (1900): "Nowhere else upon this planet are the inalienable rights of women as much appreciated as on the newly settled borders of the United States. Men have had opportunities in our remote countries to see the worth of the civilized woman who came with them or among them to new settlements after the Indian woman's day. And they have seen her, not as the parasitic woman who inherits wealth, or the equally selfish woman who lives in idleness upon her husband's toil, but as their helpmate, companion, counselor, and fellow homemaker…" Abigail knew about all of this because she had lived it intimately. Her writing was flourishing and in 1905 she published her second novel, *From the West to the West*, and in 1914 she published her book *Path Breaking: An Autobiographical History of the Equal Suffrage Movement in the Pacific Coast States*.

Over the span of forty-six years, Abigail authored twenty-two didactic novels, most written week to week under the pressure of deadlines. They were serialized in her newspapers; with heroines whose lives bore a striking resemblance to her own and taught lessons bearing on "the woman question."

Abigail believed that allegorical fiction was the strongest and most effective medium. In her *How to Win the Ballot* she enjoyed analyzing women's rhetorical situation and issued this approach: "The first fact to be considered when working to win the ballot, is that there is but one way by which we may hope to obtain it and that is by and through the affirmative votes of men…we must show them that we are inspired by the same patriotic motives that induce them to prize it … (and) impress upon all men the fact that we are not intending to interfere, in any way, with their rights; and all we ask is to be allowed to decide, for ourselves, also as to what our rights should be."

Whether Abigail was celebrating women or men, real persons or somewhat mythic frontier figures, the praise she offered always invited her to live up to the models of humanity presented in her writings, and to "become" them. Her lectures were often autobiographical as she recounted her experiences as a mother of six, a farmer and pioneer settler in Oregon, as well as a trailblazer in the movement for equal rights. The former typically outlined the unceasing toil and drudgery that were the lot of a frontier wife, while the latter emphasized her decades-long, herculean, sometimes solitary, and often ill-appreciated labors, at a great personal sacrifice.

As she grew older, Abigail often attributed her infirmities to overwork and expressed hope that she would live to see her life's work consummated. On the brink of the 1912 referendum, which was finally successful, Abigail pleaded: "I am an old woman now. The hand that pens these lines is rheumatic and feeble. The present equal suffrage campaign, launched by myself, is offered as a loving appeal to the present voters of Oregon for the enfranchisement of your mothers, wives, and sisters - I do not, myself, expect ever to be able to cast a full free ballot, but I do hope that you gentlemen, who have never been compelled to struggle for the right to vote, will vote 300 times YES and send me to heaven as a free angel."

While it is true that Abigail Scott Duniway was a controversial, opinionated, and strident advocate for women and equality, she could inspire as well as infuriate. She could be combative and always insisted on running a campaign her own way. She was not always organized or easy to get along with. These qualities may have alienated potential allies both inside and outside the movement. However, her outspoken voice and prodigious pen, her indefatigable determination, her wit, and shared wisdom, and finally her stature as a public woman, were unmatched. Even facing health issues and at an older age, she was unflagging, articulate, forceful, and always made a very strong impression. Abigail was a natural platform orator, often using a touch of sarcasm and always a dash of humor, which made her very effective. It was said of her that even as an impromptu speaker; she had few equals.

Despite her valiant efforts, her main goal of equal suffrage for women in Oregon eluded her. Abigail's efforts, however, bore fruit elsewhere. She was given much credit for the adoption of women's suffrage in Washington Territory in 1883 and in Idaho in 1896. Abigail Duniway had helped pave the way.

The passage of equal suffrage in the Pacific Northwest was largely due to her efforts and was a personal triumph. Abigail left an estate valued at $600. That, however, is not the measure of this woman's worth, as she left so much more. She left a family of sturdy sons, who were a credit to the community in which they lived and worked, as well as to the entire state of Oregon. She left the riches, memory, and legacy of a lifelong struggle to overcome obstacles and serve as a voice for those needing a voice. Abigail was an example of womanhood, motherhood, and courage that illustrates how one can rise above a common and oppressive life and become an advocate and reformer without sacrificing home ties. This is a little-known woman that must be honored and remembered.

Suggestions for further reading:

Rebel for Rights: Abigail Scott Duniway by Ruth Barnes Moynihan

Yours for Liberty: Selections from Abigail Scott Duniway's Suffrage Newspaper by Jean M. Ward and Elaine A. Maveety

From the West to the West: Across the Plains to Oregon (Classic Reprint) by Abigail Scott Duniway

Edith Olive Stratton Kitt

Photo Credit: Arizona Historical Society

"The small house in which I was born had dirt walls, a dirt floor and a dirt roof. There was only one board floor in the village and that was in the most prosperous saloon."

Edith Olive Stratton was born on December 15, 1878, in Florence, Arizona Territory. She was the daughter of Emerson Stratton of Clyde, New York, and Carrie Aines Stratton of Cotuit, Massachusetts. In her own words: "…That birth was really quite an experience for my father since I arrived, while he was scouring the town looking for the only doctor, whom he found later, drunk and playing cards in the back room of a saloon. The small house in which I was born had dirt walls, a dirt floor, and a dirt roof. (It was actually a dugout built into the side of a hill.) There was only one board floor in the entire village and that was in the most prosperous saloon where once in a while the townspeople would clear out the bar and hold dances in this saloon. All the mothers brought their babies and put them to bed on a long bench. Mother was from New England, but she did go to these dances, that was until some man sat on me. After that, she refused to go anymore."

Edith's home was thirty miles from Tucson as the crow flies, but seventy-five as the road crawled. "Mother was once on the ranch for eight months without seeing another American woman." Edith and her three siblings, Mabel, Johnny, and Elmer grew up on the ranch their father had named Pandora Ranch, after the Greek myth about a box that spilled out all the ills of the world, leaving only hope. He felt at that time, everything but hope was lost, a sentiment that has reappeared often in history.

The children had a tutor on the ranch when they could find one, and occasionally they went to the nearest public school. Sometimes in the winter, their mother would rent a house in the closest town and she and the children would stay there. During those intervals, Edith missed the ranch terribly. She really enjoyed ranch life, which included horseback riding, hunting with her father, and the semiannual roundups. It was part of her and seemed to be in her blood. Her youth was tomboyish, and she even enjoyed doing chores. She began riding as a wee baby in a sling that was made from an old tablecloth and knotted around her father's neck and shoulders. As Edith grew, she had her own horse, "Little Bill," that she rode alone or with her sister. She got her first shotgun when she was ten and hunted quail, duck, deer, and skunk. Skunk? Because she said: "skunk skins were worth fifty cents to a dollar and in one season I made fifteen dollars." She became a crack shot and often brought wild game home for dinner. Edith survived the raging flood waters of the San Pedro River, and it is said that once she sailed off in her mother's washtub across a creek. Apparently, she was rescued.

Edith's mother strongly disapproved of her daughter's wild activities, and she discouraged Edith's association with local ranch hands. Despite her mother's disapproval, the local cowboys taught Edith to make rope from cowhide and how to twist horsehair using a notched stick called a tarabilla. Edith often sighed and said she greatly regretted "not being a cowboy among cowboys." While Edith loved ranch life, her family was finding it more and more difficult to make ends meet financially. The drought in 1895, along with grasses being overgrazed, spelled financial doom for this ranching family. Eventually, they were forced to leave their beloved ranch and settled in Los Angeles. Edith graduated from the Los Angeles Normal School in 1900. She returned to Arizona to study for a while at the University of Arizona. She ended up accepting a teaching position at an old ranch school near Liberty, just southwest of Phoenix.

In 1903 Edith married George F. Kitt. The couple had a daughter, Edith, born in 1904, and a son, George Roskruge, born in 1906. While Edith's college education was interrupted by her teaching positions, subsequent marriage, and raising children, she did earn her degree after attending classes on and off at the University of Arizona. "I had been taking courses on and off for twenty years. I thought I was in school longer than anyone in the history of the university."

Edith was active in community affairs as a member of the Tucson Woman's Club, the Arizona Federation of Women's Clubs, the American Legion Auxiliary, and The Business and Professional Women's Club. She and three others organized the Tucson Fine Arts Association. Edith was always fascinated with history and particularly the history of Arizona. In 1925 she served as secretary of the Arizona Pioneers Historical Society, which at that time only had three members. The following year it rose to twenty-nine, due to her administration and leadership. Originally, membership was limited to men, but gradually women became an integral part of the organization, largely due to Edith. It was noted that she herself performed the janitorial tasks to save money for the

Historical Society. She recruited new members, collected dues, and solicited donations. "As for our collection," she said, "I guess I became a pretty good beggar. I asked authors for their new books, organizations for their published reports, and the newspaper editors of the state for free subscriptions to their dailies and weeklies. My argument was that Arizona was still making history."

It was during this time that Edith recorded her father's early memories of Arizona, just before he died. She used these recollections, along with her own, to write a book that was finally published in 1964, *Pioneering in Arizona: The Reminiscences of Emerson Oliver Stratton and Edith Stratton Kitt.* She educated herself on collection and cataloging methods by extensive reading and visiting other libraries and museums around the country. The Historical Society was then housed in a small room at the Tucsonia Hotel in Tucson. In 1955 it was moved to its current location at 949 East Second St. Edith traveled extensively collecting artifacts, relics, manuscripts, and other bits and pieces of Arizona's history. "I tried to make the office a kind of clubhouse for the old-timers," she said, "and there I took down their reminiscences. Some of these were detailed and highly factual; others had to be taken with a grain of salt." When they stopped by to chat, Edith made notes of their conversations. While they were talking, she would ask about old letters, documents, and diaries. This way, she was able to acquire and preserve many of these historical records that might otherwise have been destroyed. Edith's goal became the development of a great central repository of Arizona's history.

As word of the Historical Society spread, donations flooded in, making the collection even richer. Edith grew the organization into one of the finest and most celebrated facilities in the Southwest. She was named the "First Lady of Arizona's Territorial Centennial" in 1963 for her tireless efforts to preserve Arizona's history and many historic contributions. It was officially renamed the Arizona Historical Society in 1970. They are still a wonderful resource, and were a great help when compiling this piece about Edith.

Suggestions for further reading:

Pioneering in Arizona: The Reminiscences of Emerson Oliver Stratton and Edith Stratton Kitt, by John Alexander Carroll, Arizona Pioneers' Historical Society, 1964

Levi's & Lace Arizona Women Who Made History by Jan Cleere

Hannah Kent Schoff

Photo Credit: Pennsylvania Historical Society

"There is no criminal class of children . . . their faults come from faults of schools, church, and State"

Hannah Kent was born on June 3, 1853, in Upper Darby, Pennsylvania, the daughter of Thomas Kent and Fanny Leonard Kent. Hannah grew up in Upper Darby and Clifton Heights and was the eldest of five children. She attended Longstreth School in Philadelphia and the Waltham Church School in Massachusetts. By her own account, she had a rather ordinary childhood.

In 1873 she married Frederic Schoff, who was an engineer. Hannah was a loving wife and mother, devoting the first twenty years of married life to raising their seven children: Wilfred Harvey, born in 1874; Edith Gertrude, born in 1877; Louise, born in 1880; Leonard Hastings, born in 1884, Harold Kent, born in 1886; Eunice Margaret, born in 1890; and Albert Lawrence, born in 1894.

One May morning in 1899, while peacefully sipping a cup of coffee in her sunroom, fingers of light languidly streaming through the curtains, reading her morning paper, Hannah was infuriated to read an article entitled "A Prodigy of Crime." The article outlined the life of a child, motherless since she was two, and sent to an orphanage at that tender age.

She later became a drudge in a city boarding house, was arrested, tried in a criminal court, and sentenced to jail for starting a fire. She was branded a criminal at eight years of age! Motherless and friendless, the child was doomed to a life of unimaginable grief. Though her actions were wrong, she was only eight years old and carried a very sad history! It was at this point Hannah acted, becoming a relentless reformer and child advocate. "… the injustice in the treatment of this poor child led me to the determination to rescue her if possible and do what I should wish someone to do for my own little girl were she in a similar position."

Hannah traveled to Washington D.C. to attend the first National Congress of Mothers. It was not long before she made her voice heard within Congress and had some influence over the direction Congress took. In 1899, she organized the Pennsylvania Congress of Mothers, which was a state branch of the national organization. Three years later, Hannah was installed as president of the national body, where she put her powerful administrative talents to work. She was inspired, had a clear vision, and advocated for the establishment of parent-teacher groups in schools. Her success was manifest in 1908 when the group changed its name to the Nation Congress of Mothers and Parent Teacher Organizations. Later, it was renamed The National Parent-Teacher Association. Hannah had blazed trails!

Hannah was determined to work on behalf of young children who were being sentenced in criminal court, but also wanted to do something for the mothers of these children; something that would help them become better parents by understanding positive parenting. She believed in a two-pronged approach: supporting mothers to be better parents, nipping some of the unacceptable behaviors in the bud, and improving the court system. She knew it was a critical piece in changing the lives of many of these children. They held the first juvenile court in Philadelphia on June 14, 1901. Hannah was in attendance. She was appointed probation officer because of her investigation of the conditions of juvenile criminals in Pennsylvania.

In her investigative work at two state reformatories, Hannah discovered 16,000 homeless waifs, some of whom were accused of very serious crimes. 16,000! Unthinkable, yet there they were. She also noted that couples entering a second marriage used these reformatories as a repository for existing children they didn't want as they began their lives anew. A dumping ground for throw-away children. Hannah was horrified to learn those innocent and helpless little ones were sent to live in dire circumstances, often kept in cages like wild animals, and under the influence of adults who were hardened criminals. She discovered there were 300 to 500 children passing through these facilities every month at the whim of the presiding judge, who most likely did not know how to deal with them. Hannah shocked the public when she presented the information she had gathered during her investigation. Because of her startling exposé, a juvenile court was established, which resulted in much more effective and efficient provision for young offenders.

Hannah's passion for improved juvenile courts and probation continued through the education of lawmakers, judges, politicians, and administrators, resulting in court systems that were much more just and believed in supporting and rehabilitating juveniles, not only in her state but in three others. Hannah was now respected as an expert on this subject and was very much in demand as a speaker and trainer. She was the first woman to address the Parliament of Canada, where she trained probation officers for their work in the newly established juvenile court system.

In 1901, the Pennsylvania legislature signed into law the reforms advocated, written, and presented by Hannah. Now that her reforms were law, she continued to monitor and ensure that the newly established juvenile court functioned properly. It was only the second in the nation. Hannah served as president of the Philadelphia Juvenile Court and Probation Association and sat in every trial that was heard over an eight-year period. She strenuously recommended an increase in salary for probation officers and raised money to see this accomplished.

From 1913 to 1919, Hannah collaborated with the U.S. Bureau of Education and helped establish a federal Home Education Division. She was chair of the American Committee on the Causes of Crime in Normal Children. During this time, Hannah was also the director of the National Kindergarten Association, and she founded the Philadelphia Alliance for the Care of Babies.

Hannah published two books: The *Wayward Child*, 1915 and *Wisdom of the Ages in Bringing Up Children*, 1933

Helen Marot

"The labor unions are group efforts in the direction of democracy."

Helen Marot was born in Philadelphia, Pennsylvania, on June 9, 1865, into a very loving, cultured, and affluent Quaker family. She was schooled at home, raised to be her own person, and encouraged to think critically and independently. Her father always told her, "I want you to think for yourself, not the way I do." Helen took these words to heart and is best remembered for her tireless efforts in addressing child labor and improving the lives and working conditions of women. Helen worked in several areas during her lifetime and was passionate about all of them.

In 1893, Helen filled positions as a librarian in Philadelphia at the King Library and in Wilmington, Delaware, as a cataloger. The head librarian, Enos L. Doan, in Delaware stated: "she brought taste and literary discrimination of a high order, qualities which, besides her thorough technical training, gave her unusual efficiency in performing her duties."

From 1895 to 1896, Helen was the literary editor for the *Ladies Home Journal*. In this position, Helen answered all literary questions for the magazine and compiled a reader's guide containing over 5,000 books with 170 author summaries. No minor accomplishment.

In 1897, along with Dr. George M. Gould and Innes Forbes, Helen opened her own little library in

Philadelphia for "those interested in social and economic problems." This tiny library soon became a hub and gathering place for liberal thinkers, as well as many others. It was said to be "the center of liberal thought in Philadelphia." The Free Library of Economics and Political Science focused on issues of economic and social reform and was influenced by the socialist organization, the Fabian Society, with original Fabian Essays published in 1889, in the wake of the Match Girls' Strike. (They went on strike because of poor working conditions at the Bryant and May match factory in London, including fourteen-hour workdays, poor pay, excessive fines, and the severe health complications of working with allotropes of white phosphorus, causing phosphorus necrosis, which destroys the bone in the jaw.)

The Fabian Society is characterized by its passionate commitment to social justice and a belief in the progressive improvement of society. It has always maintained a diversity of opinion, motivated by the desire to stimulate debate, rather than to promote a particular political "line." Its publications represent only the views of its authors. In 1900, the Fabian Society joined with the trade unions to establish the

Labor Party and has remained affiliated with it ever since. From the earliest days, the Fabians influenced Labor Party's political ideas.

On June 15, 1897, the *Philadelphia Record* said of Helen's Free Library of Economics and Political Science, "Philadelphia has been enriched with a library distinctively modern and progressive in spirit. The new library forms an important supplement to the municipal system since the topics of the day, and the problems of the industrial and sociological world, cannot be thoroughly followed by an institution for the general circulation of books. With its proposed technical classification of magazine literature and an accessible collection of pamphlets and volumes, the Library of Economics should become a powerful factor for civic and social education in the community and Commonwealth." Helen shared her thoughts about the library in a statement in 1902: "It was founded on the idea that freely offered opportunities from education in economics and political science make directly for a more intelligent public opinion and a higher citizenship."

The collection was comprised of 600 books, ninety-one periodicals, and over 2,000 pamphlets. It was unique and necessary, as much of the information in this little library was not available anywhere else and met a very specific community need. To keep current with information, the library collected government publications, news clippings, reports from labor societies, and similar materials. The collection was all donated by like-minded organizations and individuals such as the American Academy of Political and Social Science, Brooklyn Institute of Arts and Sciences, Church Social Union, Civic Club of Philadelphia, Direct Legislation League, Englishwoman's Review, Fabian Society, Independent Labor Party, Indian Rights Association, Labor Exchange, and Land Nationalization League to name a few. While the collection was small, library patrons, including teachers and students, found the collections to be quite necessary, interesting, and educational. It was a rich community resource used and valued by many. Patrons could purchase books, or traditional library checkout out was available if they could not come to the reading room during regular hours.

The library was open daily from 11 am to 6 pm and on Sundays until 10 pm. It was a very popular gathering place for the reformers and socialists of Philadelphia, with both public and private lectures and classes offered. Helen served on the lectures committee. The lectures were all well attended, often with standing-room-only crowds that overflowed the rooms. Through this little library, Helen was determined to educate the people of Philadelphia in areas of social change, justice, and a more humane society. She did this with amazing courage and tenacity but also blended her approach with guileless romanticism and hardheaded realism. This made for an interesting result. The first lecture was "The Economics of Socialism," delivered by James R. MacDonald of the London Fabian Society, who was to become the Prime Minister of the United Kingdom. Other lectures followed along in the same vein. The series continued with educational, enlightening, and critical topics.

Because of Helen's passion for social issues, and her growing reputation in this area, she was hired by the United States Industrial Commission in 1899 to investigate the sewing and custom tailoring houses in Philadelphia. She was totally shocked at what she found. Working conditions were abysmal, especially for women and children. This was a real turning point in her life. These discoveries changed Helen Marot from a mild-mannered teacher and librarian to a radical and militant activist. She published an exposé, *A Handbook of Labor Literature* when she completed her investigation. Helen then went to New York City in 1902 to investigate child labor issues for the Association of Neighborhood Workers. She, with Florence Kelley and Josephine Lara Goldmark, formed the New York Child Labor Committee.

While in New York, Helen lectured and proselytized to all who would listen, on the benefits of unions to members of the garment trade. She organized a new union for bookkeepers, stenographers, and accountants. Helen was astute, thorough in her research, well-informed, and assertive in her presentations. This helped persuade the U.S. Supreme Court to uphold the constitutionality of the law, limiting the hours of a workday for women. She also authored a report on child labor in the city that was influential in passing the 1903 Compulsory Education Act by the state legislature.

Workers in the garment industry toiled in small sweatshops, for ridiculously low wages, and were often expected to work sixty-five to seventy-five hours per week, which meant ten to twelve-hour workdays. They were required to supply their own basic materials, including needles, thread, and sometimes even sewing machines. Management levied a fine for tardiness or damage to a piece of clothing.

At some worksites, such as the Triangle Shirtwaist Company, steel doors were used to lock employees in to prevent them from taking breaks. This resulted in the women having to ask a supervisor for permission to use a restroom, which was an outhouse at the rear of the building. The New York Shirtwaist Strike, which highlighted the plight of the working women in the garment industry, and empowered them to begin an industrial revolution, led to the formation of the International Ladies Garment Workers.

On December 3, 1909, Helen and five other women, Mary Dreier, Ida Rauh, Rena Borky, Yetta Raff, and Mary Effers, marched to City Hall, demanding an end to abuse, and establishing better working conditions. The strike began with sixteen women, but eventually, 41,000 brave women walked off the job. They stayed out for fourteen weeks until some of their demands for better conditions were met. In the end, they made a considerable impact. Their voices were heard!

On March 25, 1911, tragedy struck. It was a Saturday afternoon, and there were 600 factory workers at the New York City Triangle Shirtwaist Company when a fire began in a rag bin. It was one of the most infamous incidents in American industrial history. The factory was on the top three floors of the Asch Building in Manhattan, which was an eight-story building. It was a sweatshop employing young, mostly immigrant women. They worked in cramped, poorly lit spaces, with even worse air quality. Most workers were teenage girls, many of whom didn't speak English. There were four elevators with access to the factory floor, but only one was operational. Workers had to find their way down a long, narrow hallway to reach it. There were two stairways that led to the street, but as previously disclosed, they locked one from the outside to prevent theft and unauthorized breaks. The fire escape was rickety and narrow and would have taken hours for all workers to use it as a method of escape, even under the best of circumstances.

The manager attempted to use a fire hose to put the fire out, but the hose was rotted, and the valve was rusted closed. They could access no water. The fire grew and panic and pandemonium ensued. The scene grew more desperate by the moment. The building was a tinderbox. Workers tried to use the elevator, but it could only hold a dozen people, and after four trips, it broke down, surrounded by heat and flames. Some girls who were waiting for the elevator grew desperate and threw themselves down the shaft to their deaths. Equally tragic, the girls who attempted to flee by the stairwells found a locked door at the bottom of the stairs. Many were burned alive on the spot and others died from smoke inhalation. In a last desperate move, others just flung themselves out of windows to a certain death.

Firefighters arrived at a horrible scene that could have been prevented. The youthful bodies of the jumpers fell onto the fire hoses, making it doubly difficult to fight the fire. In addition, the ladders of the firefighters only reached seven floors. The fire began on the eighth floor and was spreading at an alarming rate. They attempted to use a net, but when unfurled to catch jumpers, three girls jumped at once and the rotted net ripped. More unnecessary death. Eighteen minutes was all it took. Eighteen horrific minutes! Forty-nine workers had burned to death, suffocated by smoke. Thirty-six were dead in the elevator shaft, and fifty-eight more died jumping to the sidewalks. Two more died a day or so later from injuries they sustained. One hundred and forty-five people perished tragically and senselessly that day.

There was a great deal of evidence that concluded positively that the owners and management of the building had been terribly negligent. The grand jury failed to indict them on manslaughter charges. The massacre for which they were responsible, finally compelled the city to enact reform. Long overdue, but at least reform was now on the table.

In 1912, Helen was part of a commission that investigated the fire. In 1913, she resigned from all her work with the trade unions and devoted herself to writing with a focus on the labor movement. The fire devastated Helen. In 1914 she published "*American Labor Unions,*" a work on the Syndicalist Industrial Workers of the World. (Syndicalism is a revolutionary doctrine by which workers seize control of the economy and government by direct means). Later, Helen served on the editorial board of *The Masses*, which was a radical journal. She also served on the staff of *The Dial*, a transcendental publication, and was a member of the U.S. Industrial Relations Committee. Otherwise, Helen lived a quiet life out of the public eye.

Idawalley "Ida" Lewis Wilson

Photo Credit: Courtesy of the National Archives, Bradley Collection

"The light is my child, and I know when it needs me, even if I sleep."

Idawalley "Ida" Lewis was born on February 25, 1842, in Newport, Rhode Island, to Captain Hosea Lewis and Zorada Willey Lewis. In 1854, the family moved to the Lime Rock Light, which is a lighthouse off the coast of Newport. Ida's father accepted the post there as Keeper of the Light. He was most likely chosen because he knew the Light already, as he had been servicing it for years.

The first tower on the site was built of stone by Captain Dutton in 1854 and was serviced by Hosea Lewis, who rowed to the rock each day. The building was a square granite tower built on Lime Rock, hence its name, and was equipped with six Fresnel lenses. The Fresnel lens is a succession of concentric rings, each consisting of an element of a simple lens assembled in a proper relationship on a flat surface to provide a short focal length. The Fresnel lens is used particularly in lighthouses and searchlights, concentrating the light into a relatively narrow beam.

The lighthouse was 300 yards from the south shore of Newport, and always completely inaccessible by land. Therefore, Ida learned to swim and row a boat very early in her life. The daily job of rowing her siblings to and from land to attend school fell to her. Ida was a strong swimmer and developed great upper-body strength. Little did she know then how well both things would serve her later in life.

The family had been settled into the lighthouse only a few months when Hosea was completely disabled by a stroke. His wife and children, primarily Ida, were able to keep up the work and duties of his position. Twelve-year-old Ida helped her mother tend the lamp in that short stone tower that was so critical to keeping boats safe along the rocky shore. They had to climb up the tower at dusk and again at midnight, to fill the lamp with oil, trim the wick, polish carbon off the reflectors, and then again to extinguish the light at dawn.

Zorada cared for Hosea, who was completely incapable of doing anything for himself, as well as caring for an invalid daughter, Harriet. Hosea and Zorada had six children, including one from Hosea's marriage with his first wife, who had died. Ida was the third oldest child, but one older brother had died and the other had left home by the time the Light Keeper Lewis suffered his stroke. Therefore, much of the responsibilities of daily life and tending the Light fell to Ida.

It wasn't long before Ida became famous for her daring rescues at sea. The first was in 1854 when four boys who were sailing near Lime Rock capsized their small boat. She saw this happen and set off in her rowboat. One by one, she plucked them over her boat's stern, out of the frigid waters, saving their lives. She was twelve years old. At the tender age of sixteen, Ida pretty much assumed all the duties at the station, becoming Lighthouse Keeper in everything but name. She was a strong and very skilled rower. Her brother, Rudolph, used to brag that "Ida knows how to handle a boat, she can hold one to windward in a gale better than any man I ever saw wet an oar. Yes, and do it too when the sea is breaking over her!" It was not fancy, but fact.

On March 29, 1869, Ida's mother saw a boat capsize in the harbor and called for Ida to offer assistance. Ida, who had been suffering from a cold and was resting in bed, jumped into action wearing just a light dress, without even grabbing a coat or shoes. It took almost fifteen minutes to launch the boat with the help of her younger brother, who went with her on this mission due to the violent nature of the storm. It seems two soldiers, Sgt. James Adams and Pvt. John McLaughlin had started from Newport out to Fort Adams under the guidance of a small, fourteen-year-old boy when their craft was swamped in the harbor as a snowstorm was churning the waters. The boy perished almost immediately, but the soldiers were able to cling to the wreckage until Ida arrived to rescue them. With the help of her younger brother, Ida was able to pull them to safety. When she reached them, she heard one of the soldiers say, "It's only a girl." The shock of seeing Ida caused him to lose his grip on the overturned boat and he sank beneath the icy water. When he popped back up to the surface after a few seconds, Ida grabbed him by the hair and hauled him over the side of her boat. The second man was so cold he couldn't move at all. She grabbed him as well and pulled him into the boat. The waves were breaking over her and threatened to swamp the small craft again and again. Ida's brother kept bailing, and they eventually reached the lighthouse safely, but wet and very cold, with two half-drowned men.

Following the 1869 rescue, a reporter from the *New York Tribune* showed up at the Lighthouse to record the events. Other articles soon appeared in *Harper's Weekly* and *Leslie's Magazine*, among others. Of course, there were those who disapproved of Ida. It is, after all, extremely easy to sit back and criticize. There were some heated and hearty debates as to whether her activities were 'properly feminine.' At the time, it was deemed unladylike for a woman to row boats. Her response was absolutely golden: "None but a donkey would consider it 'un-feminine,' to save lives."

Later, during an interview, Ida recalled that she needed all her months and years of exercise and rowing experience for that day. It was later reported in an edition of the *Providence Journal* that the soldiers had been imbibing in a long evening of liquid refreshment at a local pub before setting out to sea. *Harper's Weekly* published an article about the heroic rescue and Ida soon became famous across the nation. The soldiers were so grateful (and didn't mind even a little bit that it had been 'just a girl' who had rescued them) that they sent Ida a gold watch.

The people of Newport gave Ida a new boat the following Independence Day, which was declared Ida Lewis Day. A parade was held in her honor and the new boat was christened *Rescue*. It was a sleek, mahogany rowboat with red velvet cushions, gold braid around the gunwales, and gold-plated oar locks. Ida also received a rare and treasured Congressional Gold Medal for lifesaving, the first woman ever to receive such an honor. The Life Saving Benevolent Association of New York sent her a silver medal.

Ida's father, Hosea, although disabled and in a wheelchair, was quite entertained by counting the number of people who came to visit the island and see Ida. He recorded there were 100 visitors per day. In one summer alone, there were 9,000 visitors. Ida received numerous gifts, letters, and marriage proposals.

In 1870, Ida accepted a proposal of marriage from Captain William Heard Wilson of Black Rock, Connecticut. Both were twenty-eight at the time of the marriage. Few details are recorded, and little is known about this event. During the marriage, she left her post and went to live back on the mainland as a concession to her husband, as he did not wish to spend his days at the Lighthouse. They separated after two years. From then on, Ida spent most of her life alone at Lime Rock. It appears the separation was amicable, as she did use "Lewis Wilson" as her last name. Perhaps the Lime Rock Light and the ocean were just too much a part of her life to leave for good. Ida Lewis became the best-known Lighthouse Keeper of her day. She kept no records of her life-saving exploits, but her fame spread quickly.

Ida's father died in 1872 and her mother, Zorada, was appointed the official Keeper of the Light. However, Zorada's health was failing fast. She had cancer. Ida went on record officially, assuming the housekeeping and caregiving duties, as well as full responsibility for the Light. When Ida's mother died, Ida was able to finally claim a title she had certainly earned.

In 1879, largely because of the influence of an admirer, General Ambrose Everett Burnside, a Civil War hero who became a Rhode Island governor and a United States Senator, the title of Keeper of the Lime Rock Lighthouse became officially Ida's. Her salary was $750 per year. She was, for a time, the highest-paid Lighthouse Keeper in the nation. Her extra earnings were given "in consideration of the remarkable services of Mrs. Wilson in the saving of lives."

Ida became a life beneficiary of the Carnegie Hero Fund, receiving a monthly pension of $30. The fund was set up by Andrew Carnegie, who put her on his private pension list. Ida put the money in the bank for her brother Rudolph, who was her assistant at Lime Rock. At one point Ida was asked where she found the strength to pull off these daring rescues. She replied, "I don't know, I ain't particularly strong. The Lord Almighty gives it to me when I need it, that's all. He can do anything you know." It is a well-known fact that a Lighthouse Keeper is frequently in harm's way, to rescue those in trouble at sea and in danger of drowning. Ida put herself in danger habitually without even thinking.

In 1889, Ida saw a fisherman fall overboard from his small boat. When she reached him, she was very surprised to discover that it was her seventy-year-old Uncle Henry Lewis, returning from a fishing trip. She got him to safety.

On August 4, 1909, five girls were leisurely rowing around Newport Harbor. A 425-foot steamship, the Commonwealth, weighing a bit more than 17 tons was leaving the harbor on its way to New York. The ship was noted for the elegance and comfort of her passenger accommodations, which included gas lighting, steam heating, and an "enchantingly beautiful" domed roof in her upper saloon. Her stability of motion led her captain to describe the Commonwealth as the finest rough-weather steamboat ever built in the United States. However, the wake from it was less than elegant for the young women in a simple rowboat. It swamped the girl's boat and quite unceremoniously dumped them all into the water. Sixty-eight-year-old Ida heard their cries for help, launched her boat *Rescue,* and pulled them out of the turbulent sea.

Perhaps one of Ida's more bizarre rescues was when she saved the life of a sheep. It was extremely stormy and the animal panicked, plunging into the cold sea, very frightened and confused. Three men attempted to rescue the sheep, but they too got into trouble in the turbulent water. Rumor has it that they had been fortifying themselves against the storm with generous libations before the attempted rescue. Fortunately, Ida was able to save all four.

During her lifetime Ida was called "the Bravest Woman in America." She met President Ulysses S. Grant, and Vice-President Schuyler Colfax when they ventured out to Lime Rock to meet her. Grant was quoted by the *Providence Journal* as having said upon his arrival at the lighthouse, "I have come to see Ida Lewis. And to see her I'd get wet up to my armpits if necessary." Also visiting the Rock were General William Tecumseh Sherman, and Admiral George Dewey. The Admiral was a frequent visitor, and Ida named her little dog Dewey after him. It is not certain how he felt about that!

Members of the women's suffrage movement, including Elizabeth Cady Stanton, came to visit Ida and frequently used her in their campaigns as an example, citing the inherent strength of women. Ida Lewis hats and scarves were sold, and at least two pieces of music were named for her: "the Ida Lewis Waltz," and "the Rescue Polka Mazurka."

Ida Lewis kept the Light for fifty-four years. She was officially credited with saving eighteen lives. Other sources, however, claim the number was much higher. Apparently, Ida was very adept and successful with rescues, but not a great record keeper. Lighthouse Board Secretary William Windom stated that "the papers before the Department, in this case, cite the instances of no less than thirteen persons saved by you from drowning, and it is stated that there are many more who do not appear in the record." It has been recorded in other sources, unofficially, that she saved as many as thirty-six from drowning.

Ida continued with her brave and valiant rescues, until she was well advanced in years, including rescuing a friend who fell overboard while rowing out for a visit. Regardless of the exact number of rescues, her career is a stellar example of the Coast Guard's core values of honor, respect, and devotion to duty. Ida stood watch through weather fair and foul, saving numerous lives in the process.

Ida Lewis is one of the most famous personages to have ever served in the Coast Guard, or in her case, the U.S. Lighthouse Service, one of the Coast Guard's predecessors. She gained national notoriety during a time when most women in the United States were not in the professional workforce or on the national stage. She overcame the biases of the time, through skill and professional ability, to become the official keeper of the Lime Rock Light Station, a position she held until her death. Ida dedicated her life to the safety of others and most certainly is a role model for both men and women serving in the Coast Guard.

In 1910 the U.S. Life Saving Service introduced a new motor lifeboat to its fleet. It was a thirty-six-foot craft made of mahogany. When the Brenton Point lifesaving station received the first one of the new boats, they named it after Ida Lewis.

The Rhode Island legislature officially changed the name of the Lime Rock Lighthouse to the Ida Lewis Rock Lighthouse in 1924. It has been noted that this is the only such honor ever paid to a Keeper of the Light in the United States.

The United States Coast Guard named the first of a new class of buoy tenders for Ida Lewis in 1995. The lead ship of the 175-foot class buoy tender of the USCGC, the Ida Lewis (WLM-551), is currently stationed in Newport Rhode Island.

The folk song "Lighthouse Keeper" by Neptune's Car was inspired by the experiences of women lighthouse tenders including Ida Lewis, Katherine Walker, and Abbie Burgess.

Ida Lewis was also celebrated in the 2002 book *The Keeper of Lime Rock: The Remarkable True Story of Ida Lewis.*

Marian Gagnon produced a documentary film in September 2014 about Ida Lewis's life, entitled "America's Forgotten Heroine," that aired on PBS. "I'm not sure why she's forgotten, but I really wanted to resuscitate her story and return her to her rightful place in history," said Gagnon. "She was this little slip of a woman, but she was fearless." In 2017, on her 175th birthday, Ida Lewis was again honored by the Coast Guard in a tweet.

Suggestions for further reading:

Lighthouse Keeper's Daughter: The Remarkable True Story of American Heroine Ida Lewis by Lenore Skomal

Rowing to The Rescue: The Story of Ida Lewis, Famous Lighthouse Heroine by Doris Licameli

Women Who Kept the Lights: An Illustrated History of Female Lighthouse Keepers by Mary Louise Clifford and J. Candace Clifford

Jessie Annette Jack Hooper

Photo Credit: Wisconsin Historical Society

"War will not end war. No matter who wins, everybody loses...War is entirely emotional. It is insanity."

Jessie Annette Jack was born on a farm in Winneshiek County, Iowa on November 9, 1865. Her mother was Mary Elizabeth Nelings and her father was David Hayes Jack, a wealthy businessman who joined a military unit from Iowa and fought during the Civil War. The couple married when David returned home from the war. Jessie's early education was with a governess.

In 1888, Jessie married Ben Hooper, an Oshkosh, Wisconsin attorney, who encouraged activism and civic interests. The couple moved to Oshkosh, where Jessie began a new chapter in her life. Even before women could vote, Mr. Hooper went to great lengths to share his right to vote with his wife. In one election he would vote as he saw fit, but in the next election, he would vote according to his wife's wishes. One can only surmise that life at the Hooper house was pretty egalitarian and full of interesting debate and conversation. The couple had one daughter, Lorna.

In 1893, Jessie and Lorna attended the International Conference for Women in Chicago. They both listened with rapt attention to a speech by Susan B.

Anthony. It impressed Jessie. She was still very shy and reluctant to hold any position of responsibility in a civic organization. In 1908, at her husband's urging, she accepted the nomination to fill a vacancy within the local chapter of Daughters of the American Revolution. Despite her reticence, Jessie won the election by a wide margin and held many other positions of leadership.

Jessie was emerging as an activist and her focus was improving healthcare options and facilities. It was an uphill battle, but one that she fought hard. She observed that men were reluctant to buy into any initiatives until they had seen success. "We found men in charge of our city government, while always polite to us, had little interest in what we wanted because we had no votes. I soon tired of joining pilgrimages to officials where we rarely got what we asked for and decided to concentrate my efforts on securing the vote for women." With many other like-minded women, Jessie joined a variety of progressive movements in Oshkosh. She was tired of attempting to dig a hole with a teaspoon when what they needed was a steam shovel, so she threw all her energies into the women's suffrage movement.

Jessie was active in the local Women's Club, and the Wisconsin Federation of Women's Clubs, and was on the executive board of the National American Women's Suffrage Association. When the marches began, she remained active, but also returned to her home state of Iowa to deliver the first "street" speech ever made by a woman. Jessie had come into her own. From there she went on to Washington D.C., where she worked alongside the leaders of the movement. Together, they would help secure the passage of the Nineteenth Amendment, giving women their precious right to vote. The button they made read, "I MARCH FOR FULL SUFFRAGE JUNE 7TH, WILL YOU?"

Jessie Hooper, along with her daughter Lorna, attended the great "Parade for Suffrage" in Chicago on June 7, 1916. It was held during the Republican National Convention. On that day, Chicago experienced the most dreadful storm they had known in years. The heavens opened and torrential rains poured non-stop, and the wind howled, living up to the nickname "the windy city." More than 5,000 suffrage supporters gathered and marched in that parade. What a bonding experience for mother and daughter, and how very exciting it must have been for them to march together, with all the other suffragists.

The group set out at the appointed hour, just as scheduled, and fell in line together wearing raincoats over their white dresses. They carried umbrellas to protect them when the wind allowed, which wasn't often. Marching mile after mile to the Coliseum where the Republican Convention was being held, they poured into the building, just in time to hear an antisuffragist statement delivered to the convention explaining that women did not want the vote! One can only imagine this caused more than one chuckle from the women marching, and now soaked to the skin. In the morning, they took the train home. Jessie was still wearing her button which said, "I MARCH FOR SUFFRAGE ON JUNE 7th, WILL YOU?"

A male fellow passenger on the train, noticing her pin, asked Jessie, "Did you march in that parade?" "Yes," she proudly replied." He then continued, "My partner and I were seated by a hotel window on Michigan Avenue when we heard, in all that frightful storm, a band playing. We knew the fireman's parade had been called off because of the ghastly weather and we simply could not imagine what it was. Looking out again, my partner said, 'my God, those women are marching in all this storm. If they want the bloody vote as badly as that, they surely ought to have it!'"

During the fight for the passage of the Nineteenth Amendment, Jessie was elected to serve as president of the National League of Women Voters (NLWV). In this leadership role, she worked to promote a variety of laws in Wisconsin, including the equal guardianship law, an increase in mother's pensions (without an adult male income, the model of military pensions was used, and they argued that a mother deserved a government pension for her service to the state through childrearing) and a law that permitted women to serve as jurors. In 1922, when Jessie retired from her position as president of NLWV, the Democratic Party of Wisconsin unanimously selected her to run as their candidate for the U.S. Senate.

Women in the press bolstered Jessie's campaign, often hosting meetings in family living rooms. The campaign rallying cry became "Whoop for Hooper." Her election platform championed the League of Nations, Veterans' compensation, and world peace. It was an auspicious platform. By this time, Jessie was a grandmother and an unpaid secretary and partner in her husband's business. He was one of only two men who donated any money to her campaign. Nominating a woman was a bold and enlightened move for the party, but most likely not popular.

Though Jessie lost the race to Robert LaFollette, she made history when she secured an amazing sixteen percent of the vote. Whoop for Hooper! After her run for the Senate, Jessie remained very visible and vocal in the political sphere. As a member of the League of Women Voters for International Cooperation to Prevent War, she fought for world peace.

During World War I, Jessie was active in Red Cross work, Liberty Loan drives, and food conservation. She also chaired the Indian Affairs Committee of the Wisconsin League of Women Voters and was an advocate for Native Americans, the Menominee Tribe in particular. She traveled to the World Disarmament Conference in Geneva, Switzerland, presenting a petition that sought the reduction of deadly weapons after World War I.

In 1933, Jessie campaigned for the United States' entry into the World Court and founded the National Conference on the Cause and Cure of War. This woman was dedicated, and passionate, working tirelessly for the causes she believed in. Jessie Annette Jack Hooper must not remain in obscurity!

Catherine Ann "Kate" Barnard

"...I stood at the mouth of a burning coal mine. Fire leaped high through the only entrance. Fifteen men were hopelessly cut off below."

Catherine Ann "Kate" Barnard was born on May 23, 1875, in Geneva, Nebraska to John P. and Rachel Sheill Barnard. Soon after her birth, the family moved to northwestern Kansas. Kate's mother died when she was only eighteen months old. Kate's father, grief-stricken and overwhelmed, left Kate in the care of relatives and neighbors.

In 1891, when she was sixteen, Kate joined her father on his ranch in Oklahoma. Her father was a jack of all trades, including a lawyer, surveyor, and postal worker. He was away a good deal of the time in Oklahoma City and other places. Kate was often left alone, working on his claim of 160 acres in Newalla. She must have been very lonely and confessed to dreams of accomplishing some "bold and heroic" deed to win her father's love and approval. Although one might think working a 160-acre claim by herself was rather bold and heroic, it seems she had her sights set higher.

Two years later Kate moved to Oklahoma City, where she attended St. Joseph's Academy, earning a teaching certificate. Kate taught in rural schools for a while, though she felt teaching didn't suit her well.

She was disillusioned and restless. She then took a stenographer training course in hopes of finding something that fit her better. This didn't do the trick either.

In 1901, using some of her local contacts, Kate worked in several clerical patronage jobs. She was eventually appointed clerk for the Democratic Party in the Oklahoma territorial legislature at Guthrie. This was her first taste of politics. Kate settled into the role, and it finally felt right.

In 1904, Kate went to the St. Louis World's Fair. She was selected from among 500 applicants to work as a territorial hostess for the Oklahoma Commission. Kate had grown up in a very rural environment, and in some ways, had led a quite sheltered existence. While in St. Louis, she experienced considerable culture shock, as she witnessed poverty, unemployment, and horrific working conditions. Kate had been unaware these conditions existed. She met with and listened to discussions by social science experts that were suggesting potential solutions to urban problems. It was here that Kate was introduced to Jane Adams, the co-founder of Hull

House, a settlement house in Chicago, serving European immigrants. Together, they toured the crime-ridden and filthy slums of the city. Kate took this all in. It was the beginning of her brilliant career as a reformer.

Upon returning home, Kate noticed things of which she previously had been unaware, such as a band of indigents in her very own town. She vowed to get legislation passed to protect Oklahoma from poverty, unemployment, and further development of slums, along with eliminating the horrible working conditions before they reached the levels she had witnessed in St. Louis. Kate was on a mission now.

In 1906, when statehood was imminent in Oklahoma, Kate entered the political arena. She wrote a series of well-researched and persuasive articles for the *Daily Oklahoman*, where she outlined the deplorable working conditions, child labor abuses, and basic human rights violations she had witnessed in St. Louis. Kate's purpose was to educate Oklahomans and warn them about the slum districts that were developing there. She thought that they needed an ounce of prevention.

Kate's efforts culminated in donations of food and clothing (over 10,000 garments) for the less fortunate. Kate was appointed to direct the newly formed Provident Association of Oklahoma City. In this position, she could bring relief to hundreds of families in need and ensure their children attended school. She even bought books for the children with her own funds.

Feeling the need to extend her work into other areas, Kate organized those who were unemployed into the Federal Labor Union, securing its connection with the American Federation of Labor. She believed all they needed was, "justice and the chance to do an honest day's work for a fair wage." In 1908, Kate attended the Shawnee Convention, which was a gathering of the Oklahoma Farmers Union, the American Federation of Labor (AFL), and four of the railroad brotherhoods. Kate, as a delegate of the AFL, urged the abolishment of child labor and encouraged the initiation of compulsory education. Kate delivered an address at the Convention that railed against child labor. Her speech was later described as, "one of the notable events of that historic body." At first, the legislators viewed Kate as a novelty, but it wasn't long before she became a power broker in the Democratic party. She impressed the party leaders and had their full attention and respect. They adopted her reform proposals for their platform at the constitutional convention just a year later. Because she was a woman, Kate could not be a delegate at the convention, but she could address the gathering. And she did just that, in a most impassioned and formidable way!

Kate had a major role in writing the Oklahoma State Constitution. With her urging, an elective office of Commissioner of Charities and Corrections was also created, for which she vigorously campaigned. Employing her great personal appeal, along with her eloquent and persuasive speaking style, she won a leadership seat on the commission in 1912. At thirty-two Kate was the first woman to win a major statewide elective office by an all-male electorate. One newspaper reporter wrote in retrospect, "This little ninety-six-pound bunch of nerves held more political power in the state of Oklahoma than any man in either party." Not only did she defeat her opponent, Republican Haxel Tomlinson, and the socialist candidate, Kate Richards O'Hara, she did it by over 35,000 votes. This was more votes than the state's first governor, Charles Haskell, garnered! People were calling her "Oklahoma Kate" as she championed the rights of the citizens of Oklahoma. She served two, four-year terms. During this time, Kate created a lasting body of reform legislation that improved conditions for the mentally ill, convicts, and laborers. Her efforts improved unsafe working conditions in the mines and resulted in safety inspections. Her legislative efforts also banned blacklisting union members and created state pension support for the widows of laborers.

Representing five Native American Tribes, Kate launched a full-scale investigation into the Indian land scandals that involved defrauding Indian minors of their timber and farmlands, along with their oil and gas rights, leaving them impoverished.

Kate continued her advocacy by organizing a chapter of the Women's International Union Label League. She became the union's representative of the Oklahoma City Trades and Labor Association. Kate lobbied to raise the minimum wage from $1.25 to

$2.25 a day. In 1909, Oklahoma passed a child labor bill written by Kate. In 1905, she became the administrator of the United Way, traveling to the slums, factories, and sweatshops of the East Coast to see firsthand what was happening there and to learn what eastern states were doing to protect working women and children.

Kate hoped to use the strategies that worked well in her own home state. On one fact-finding mission, she witnessed a horrific incident at a coal mine and was impacted by the scene. "... I stood at the mouth of a burning coal mine. Fire leaped high through the only entrance. Fifteen men were hopelessly cut off below. The smell of their burning flesh came up to us on the crest of the flame. A woman, clothed in only one garment, with three children clinging to it, and a babe in her arms, peered into the pit. Her husband was below. She cried out, and going suddenly insane, tried to leap down to join him. There was only one reason why that mine should have but one entrance; it would cost money to provide another. Then and there I decided to consecrate myself to the remedy."

Kate advocated for better conditions for mine workers. She encouraged labor forces to demand an eight-hour workday for miners, install a labor commissioner, and chief mine inspector, as well as health and safety measures for laborers and compensation for those miners injured on the job.

During her second term in 1911, Kate launched a comprehensive investigation into widespread fraud in the court-ordered administration of guardianship for orphaned Indian minors. The land was ceded by the federal government to Native Americans and held in a trust, which was governed by guardians and directed by the probate court. Kate went on to discover that a great deal of exploitation had occurred. She found one guardian who had over fifty children in custody, although he did not know where any of them were. Kate's work disclosed that the Oklahoma probate court system was rotten to the core and overrun with graft and corruption. She was the only one at the time to step up and defend the rights of Indian youth who were being cheated out of their rights and land. Kate handled the restoration of over one million dollars to the Native American communities.

This work raised the ire of William H. Murray and other wealthy and prominent Oklahoma businessmen and officials. Just who did Kate think she was defending the Indians, and her, a woman at that?! What resulted was that these wealthy and powerful men convinced the state legislature to defund her office. This ended her political career, but not her work as a reformer. In 1993, Wilma Mankiller included a quote from Kate Barnard in her book, *Mankiller, A Chief, and Her People*: "I have been compelled to see orphans robbed, starved, and burned for money. I have named the men and accused them and furnished the records and affidavits to convict them, but with no result. I decided long ago that Oklahoma had no citizen who cared whether or not an orphan is robbed or starved or killed because his dead claim is easier to handle than if he were alive."

Kate's investigation into the treatment of over 300 Oklahoma prisoners held in a Kansas prison, because their home state had no prison, made national headlines, and further enhanced her reputation as a reformer. Evidence of deplorable conditions was found and exposed. There were many cases of maltreatment that were finally acknowledged. Prisoners were overworked and subjected to inhumane punishments. Kate wrote a scathing report. She advocated for reform that would put psychopathic prisoners in hospitals for care and put other prisoners to work at the same rate of pay they would receive if not in prison.

Educational systems were put into place in prisons, along with establishing worksites for released prisoners to help with their reentry into society. In McAlester, Oklahoma, these efforts resulted in the construction of their own penitentiary, the repatriation of convicts, and the creation of a wide range of reforms. A three-tier state prison system was created that comprised a penitentiary, a reformatory, and a boy's training school.

Oddly enough, one issue Kate did not fight for was women's suffrage. She believed that when enough women in Oklahoma wanted the right to vote, the men would grant it to them. Her father had not approved of suffrage and maybe some of his attitudes had rubbed off on her. Who knows? Regardless, Kate didn't oppose the right of women to vote. She was simply not going to lead the charge on that one.

Kate was inducted into the Oklahoma Women's Hall of Fame in 1982.

In 1999, the Oklahoma Commission on the Status of Women established the Kate Barnard Award to honor women in public service.

In 2001, a statue of Kate Barnard was dedicated in the state capitol building.

Suggestions for further reading:

Kate Barnard: Oklahoma's good angel (Oklahoma statesmen series) by Bob Burke and Glenda Carlille

One Woman's Political Journey: Kate Barnard and Social Reform, 1875–1930 by Lynn Musslewhite and Suzanne Jones Crawford

Laura Gilpin

Photo Credit: New Mexico History Museum, Palace of the Governors

"Much earnest philosophical thought is born of the life which springs from close association with nature."

Laura Gilpin, the daughter of Emma and Frank Gilpin, was born on April 22, 1891, in Colorado Springs, Colorado. Frank first came west in 1880 to help his brother, Bernard, with a business venture - The Maryland Cattle Company - but the winter of

1886 was disastrous and wiped out the burgeoning cattle business. This setback sent Frank scrambling for work and began a lifelong pattern of moving from one job to another. He would become an adventurer, cowboy, miner, investor, manager of a hotel and a mine, as well as a cattle rancher. Frank believed that the west was full of opportunity and possibility, both of which seemed to elude him. It wasn't until the 1920s that he found his niche and settled down as a successful artisan and craftsman of fine furniture.

Laura's mother, Emma Gosler Miller, grew up in St. Louis and Chicago. Her family and the Gilpin family were friends. Frank and Emma's friendship culminated in marriage on April 26, 1890, after a long courtship. Frank convinced Emma to leave her cultured and comfortable life in the east and move to the wilds of the Rocky Mountains. While she agreed, Emma did not share her husband's passion for the western way of life.

Emma was raised in a rich cultural environment and educated at very proper schools. When she and Frank settled at their Horse Creek Ranch, she was very homesick. Emma longed for the cultural stimulation she was accustomed to. While living in the wilds of the west, she always attempted to bring some culture and refinement to the rustic homesteads. This took on many forms. When she was expecting Laura, Emma traveled sixty-five miles to the home of an acquaintance, in Austin Bluffs, to be closer to a doctor. She was determined to receive the best care for herself and her baby, this included a safe place for the birth with proper attendants. Emma did not consider Horse Creek Ranch the best place to give birth to her first child!

Quite unlike her mother, Laura thrived and embraced the western way of life. As a child, she loved the outdoors and exploring. Her father encouraged her to hike and camp in the untamed Colorado landscape. Laura was distantly related to William Gilpin, the 19th-century explorer who became the first territorial governor of Colorado, and to William Henry Jackson, the renowned photographer, and painter. As a young girl, her family was friends with the English physician, Dr. William A. Bell. Along with being a physician, Dr. Bell was also the photographer for the Kansas and Pacific Railroad during 1867.

Another of Laura's friends was William Jackson Palmer, an engineer, Civil War General, and the founder of the town of Colorado Springs. He also founded the Denver and Rio Grande Railroad. William was elderly when Laura knew him, but he had a great fondness for Laura, and often took her horseback riding. As they rode the countryside, William pointed out various plants, trees, and wildlife, telling Laura their names. She recalls, "He taught me to know the outdoors, and especially to love it." Laura thrived under William's tutelage and attributed her lifelong passion and dedication for photography to him.

On Laura's twelfth birthday, she received a Brownie camera as a gift from her parents. The following year, she received a developing tank. Laura loved photography, mastering the early color photographic process. She taught herself by following the directions that were enclosed in the supplies. Laura's talent was very evident. She was blossoming as a photographer, making still-life prints from simple subjects she found around the farm.

The following year, Laura used that little Brownie camera to photograph the St. Louis World's Fair. She often said this was a very important year in her life. While in St. Louis, Laura visited her friend and namesake, "Laura" Perry, who was blind. Together, they visited the fair daily for a month and Laura Gilpin was Laura Perry's eyes, describing even minute details for her. "The experience taught me the observation I would have never learned otherwise," Laura Gilpin mused.

Laura acquired most of her education in the East, from 1905 to 1909. (Her mother was insistent that Laura receive a formal education at Eastern boarding schools). First, Laura attended Baldwin's School in Bryn Mawr, Pennsylvania, followed by a stint at the Rosemary Hill School in Greenwich, Connecticut. However, she returned home before graduating.

By 1909, Laura was making Lumiere autochrome pictures like a professional. This was a very early form of color photography, developed by two brothers in France, using glass plates, potato starch, and color. Laura's mother was so impressed with her talent, she took Laura back east to meet the amazing photographer, Gertrude Kasebier, a native of Colorado. Gertrude was also impressed with Laura's work and advised her to train professionally. Gertrude Kasebier was an American photographer known for her images of motherhood and her portraits of Native Americans. Gertrude also promoted photography as a career option for women.

The following year, hoping that her daughter would develop an interest in the violin, Emma insisted Laura study at the New England Conservatory of Music. However, around this time, there was a bit of a downturn in the family fortune. This, combined with Laura's less-than-ardent interest and mediocre talent, resulted in her return to her beloved Rockies after only a year at the Conservatory.

The Gilpin family was now living on a 1,800-acre farm in Austin, Colorado. Laura was in her element and had time to think about her life. Her dream was to study with the photographic masters of the day in New York City. In a bold endeavor, Laura became an entrepreneur. She purchased and raised 400 turkey chicks. She built secure pens and developed a special blend of feed. When the birds reached maturity, Laura butchered and dressed them. She then sold her finished product to local gourmet restaurants. Her turkey business was wildly successful. A Denver newspaper article featured her success, "Society Girl Raises 400 Turkeys." Laura eventually sold her business for $10,000. She loaned her perpetually insolvent father $9,000 to keep the family afloat, using the remaining funds to finance her education. Laura was now much closer to realizing her dream.

Laura enrolled in a twenty-eight-week course at one of the leading photographic schools, the Clarence H. White School of Photography, in New York, recommended by Gertrude Kasebier. Gertrude became a mentor and a dear friend. The teaching staff at the White school included such prominent photographers and artists as White himself, Max Weber, and Paul Anderson. The school taught photography both as a commercial tool and as a form of artistic expression. Laura admired White, calling him, "one of the greatest teachers I have ever known in any field." His theory was that taking an excellent picture involved an investment in emotion and feelings. Laura learned photographic processes, techniques, principles of composition, technical skills, and alternative printing methods that included platinum printing, a process she employed over the next sixty years.

Laura Gilpin was one of the greatest platinum printers and thought it was the most beautiful result a photographer could achieve. She said, "I have always loved the platinum printing process. It has the longest scale and one can get the greatest contrast. It's not a difficult process; it just takes time." A platinum print is made with paper containing light-sensitive iron salts and a platinum compound, rather than the conventional silver salts, and exposed in daylight in contact with a negative. William Willis invented the process in 1873 and made it commercially available in 1879.

Laura was the epitome of Western toughness, but also possessed great Eastern gentility. She often spoke with authority about the challenges of landscape photography, and often went to extreme lengths to get the desired picture. Hiring a plane or scouting out an overnight camping place was not unusual for Laura. Her first published photograph was of the Grand Canyon.

Laura spent the following summer at the White School in Colorado Springs, but in the fall, she moved back to New York City, immersing herself in study and work. In 1918, she became very ill with Spanish influenza, forcing her to return to her home in Colorado. Spanish flu, also known as the Great Influenza epidemic, or the 1918 influenza pandemic, was a deadly global pandemic caused by the H1N1 influenza A virus. Laura's mother was quite concerned about her daughter's health. To ensure a speedy and full recovery for her, Emma hired a professional nurse, Elizabeth (Betsy) Forster, to care for Laura. Betsy was working as a visiting nurse in remote Arizona. She left that position temporarily to care for Laura. It began a lifelong friendship; one of dedication, devotion, love, and sharing. Laura regained her health and Betsy resumed her duties as a visiting nurse.

Once again, Laura immersed herself in her art. Her family was very supportive. Laura's subjects included portraits of friends, family, acquaintances, and landscapes. In 1919 she joined a group of artists in Colorado Springs that were associated with the Broadmoor Art Academy where she did a series of photographic brochures for the school. This was the year that the Academy opened, founded with a vision of creating a new art institution of national stature. The Academy was in a converted mansion on the corner of Cascade and Dale in Colorado Springs, Colorado. The building had been the home of the school's founders, Spencer and Julie Penrose, who were the owners of the Broadmoor Hotel. Art instructors and students alike brought their diverse styles and talents to Colorado, lured by the exquisite landscapes that only the west affords.

After her studies at the Broadmoor Art Academy, Laura continued her art, but never went back to school. Her formal education had ended, though her career in photography was just beginning. Laura often accompanied Betsy to the far reaches of the Navajo reservations in remote areas of Arizona. It is interesting to note that Laura's relationship with the Navajo had its beginnings in 1930 when she and Betsy ran out of gas while on a camping trip. They were in a remote area of a reservation, in the middle of nowhere, twenty miles from Chinle. It was during these trips they both became totally and respectfully enamored with the Navajo people. While Betsy nursed those who needed her care, Laura photographed and wrote their stories. She had a great and enduring love and understanding of the Navajo; the love and respect were reciprocated.

Laura said, "The Navajo have two exceptional qualities that stand out, dignity and happiness." She believed that both sprung from their vital traditional faith; faith in nature and faith in themselves. The early pictures Laura took were focused on individuals, but through these portraits, she came to grasp the difference between sentimentality and sentiment. Her pictures of families, trading posts, hogans, and ceremonies created a vivid, insightful, and compassionate record of traditional Navajo life during that era.

From 1931 to 1933, Laura's photos show the Navajo community between wars, before the 20th century had transformed their traditional lifeways. Few families had automobiles, electricity, or indoor plumbing. Water had to be hauled. Most of them still made a living in the traditional way, sheepherding, or weaving, and few spoke English. This intimate work of Laura's reflects the personal relationships that she and Betsy had with the Navajo people.

This was a time in history when people recognized that rather than having painted portraits done, photography was a much easier, less expensive, and more satisfying way to achieve a similar effect. Laura practiced the Pictorial style, which imitates the effects of painting. When she was in the studio, she focused on the natural spirit of her subjects, using relaxed poses and soft, natural light. Laura exhibited her work in Copenhagen at the Photographic Salon. She also had a one woman show of sixty-one works of both portraits and landscapes at the Broadmoor in Colorado. The work from the Broadmoor show toured the Museum of New Mexico in Santa Fe and the Denver Public Library. Laura's work was also being shown in Buffalo, Pittsburgh, San Francisco, Toronto, Seattle, and New York. Laura was becoming known. She submitted portraits and still life art to exhibitions and competitions, though her genuine success stemmed from western landscape photographs. Laura had always loved the West and her appreciation for this landscape deepened when she traveled with her father to New Mexico.

Laura spent time in New York studying portrait sculpture with Brenda Putnam to improve her portrait work, to which she was very dedicated. Putnam was a noted American sculptor, teacher, and author. They were roommates, supported each other, and often had rousing discussions about art. This led to a deep and lasting friendship between the two women. They remained in close contact for the rest of their lives.

Laura later traveled to Europe, a trip that proved very impactful to her work. She experimented more with a sharp focus in her photography and was very interested in creating photographic books after they introduced her to the work of William Blake, an English poet, painter, and printmaker who was unrecognized during his life. The time Laura spent in Europe expanded her knowledge of art and art history, which helped to solidify her identity as a western American artist. Feeling more confident in who she was, and developing both her style and niche, paved the way for a deeper passion for her beloved western landscape.

To earn a living, Laura became a "contract" photographer, creating portraits and landscapes to promote business and tourism and support educational and health institutions. During the early years of the great depression (1929-1939), she created a series of picture postcards as a way of generating some income. She also published guidebooks, providing both images and text. After the attack on Pearl Harbor in 1941, the United States entered World War II. The following year Laura worked as publicity director and chief photographer for Boeing Aircraft in Wichita, Kansas, until 1945.

The subjects that Laura found the most meaningful, satisfying, and dear to her heart though, were those of the Pueblo and Navajo she photographed in their homelands when she traveled with Betsy. In New Mexico, Laura photographed Pueblo Indians and the ruins of their Anasazi ancestors, as well as the Canyon de Chelly region, near Santa Fe. In 1941 she published her first major book, *The Pueblos: A Camera Chronicle*, based on a series of lantern slides she had made of archaeological sites. Other books of her photographs are *The Pueblos* (1941), *Temples in Yucatan* (1948), and *The Rio Grande* (1949).

Laura was very interested in both the history and archeology of the region, photographing the native people and their ancient ruins. Her work during this period reflects her previous training, placing greater emphasis on the evocation of mood (Pictorialism) than on detail. She favored the soft, delicate grays of platinum printing papers. The results were stunning and live on today. Her soft-focus prints of Mesa Verde and the prairies of Colorado, show as much about the emotion the artist was feeling while viewing the scene, as the subject itself. They are inarguably gorgeous.

Laura returned to the Navajo reservation in 1950 to rephotograph many of her previous subjects for her book, *The Enduring Navajo,* published in 1968. Her photographs are characteristically infused with a luminous, soft light and composed in classic elegance. While there, Laura revisited many old friends and acquaintances. She attempted to record the current Navajo worldview, making note of the changes that had occurred since her last visit there, including political and economic issues that were now facing the tribe.

Laura Gilpin applied compassion to the relationship between the landscape and the native people, a trait that distinguished her from most male landscape photographers of the West. Many still regard her as the only significant woman landscape photographer of her time. Thus, in 1968, when her book, *The Enduring Navajo* was published, John Collier, Jr., a renowned photographer, and anthropologist said of the book, "it is a work of LOVE not ANALYSIS." It is a work that really captures Laura's deep sense of understanding and respect for the Navajo people. She focused on issues that were important to the Navajo, their culture, and their traditions. Laura's work with the Navajo remains a respected and admired record of the Dineh, (the People), and her body of work honors them.

Scholars offered much praise for Laura's record of highlighting and honoring a culture that many said was dying, perhaps in attitude and desire, similar to what Edward Curtis, the renowned ethnographer, and photographer did in his work, *A Vanishing Race*. But Laura saw a long and rich future for these people, and she did not see them as "a dying race."

Laura and her work have been recognized internationally. The finest museums continue to display her photographs. Laura was accepted as a member of the Royal Photographic Society of Great Britain in 1930. Her work has influenced many in the art field, excelling in a career that was new for women. Ansel Adams had nothing but the highest praise for Laura and her art, saying she had, "a highly individualistic eye. I don't have the sense that she was influenced except by the land itself." The scholar and critic, John Brinkerhoff Jackson, said, "Miss Gilpin's camera, like the sundial, records only the sunny hours." He bestowed lavish praise for her book, *The Enduring Navajo,* acknowledging its accurate economic, social, and agricultural data, stating, "It is far more than a picture book, therefore; it is a geography for adults."

Laura was a consummate professional and craftswoman, with an enduring love for the world around her. She wrote to a friend in 1956, "What I consider really fine landscapes are very few and far between. I consider this field one of the greatest challenges and it is the principal reason I live in the west. I am willing to drive many miles, expose a lot of film, wait untold hours, camp out to be somewhere at sunrise, make many return trips to get what I am after."

Laura continued her important work as a photographer well into her advanced years, even though crippled by arthritis. Just a few weeks before her death at age eighty-eight, she leaned out the window of a small aircraft flying low over the Rio Grande Valley, capturing what she wanted on film to make one of her last photographs.

Laura received honorary doctorates at both Colorado and New Mexico State universities, and a State Arts Award in New Mexico. The art award honored her for her achievements, "... as a photographer she has demonstrated for over fifty years that her art draws its expressive power from her compassionate attunement to her chosen subjects and her honest respect for her medium."

While highly distinguished as a young artist, Laura worked for many decades with little recognition at all. However, during the 1970s, when the interest in photographic collection peaked, Laura finally received the acclaim she deserved. Several national exhibits featured her work, and in 1975 Laura received a Guggenheim grant to make hand-coated, platinum prints; the process in which she had a lifelong interest and accomplishment.

Note: *The Enduring Navajo* is one of the most beautiful books I have ever laid my hands on. While it may be difficult to find, many larger libraries have it.

Suggestions for further reading:

The Weight of a Soul by Laura Gilpin

The Enduring Navajo by Laura Gilpin (1984-03-03)

Laura Gilpin: An Enduring Grace by Martha A. Sandweiss

Lillian Moller Gilbreth

Photo Credit: New Mexico History Museum, Palace of the Governors

"To meet today's challenge to women, one must make her own philosophy of life, have a sense of humor and be mentally alert and fit physically, mentally, and spiritually"

Lillian Moller was born on May 24, 1878, in Oakland, California. She was the second of eleven children born to Annie Delger Moller and William Moller, who was a building supply merchant. They were a well-to-do, Victorian family. Her parents named her Lillie when she was born. Later, she legally changed her name to Lillian. Because she was such a shy child, her parents educated her at home. Lillian's formal education didn't begin at a public elementary school until she was nine years old. Despite her prior education, she was required to begin again at the first-grade level, but it was not a significant setback, and she progressed rapidly.

Academically, Lillian always excelled. By the time she entered high school, she was still socially inexperienced and awkward with classmates. She dreaded the day when she would have to enter the world of dating and courtship. Boys petrified her, and she thought of herself as unattractive. While Lillian resigned herself to the idea of remaining single, she yearned for something beyond the life of a spinster. Writing, especially poetry, was a way for her to express herself. In the end, writing drew Lillian out, and thus she found comfort and acceptance with her peers.

Lillian was elected vice president of her senior class at Oakland High school. In May of 1896, she graduated with the highest grades. One of her English teachers encouraged her to pursue a literary career. She had ultimately excelled in high school and now felt more confident. Lillian had her heart set on studying music and literature. Her father did not believe in higher education for women, feeling they needed just enough knowledge to be good wives and mothers, and to manage a home successfully with grace and ease.

Lillian persuaded him to let her begin her studies at the University of California, Berkeley since one of her cousins was already studying there. He insisted she must live at home and keep up with all her household duties. Lillian commuted by streetcar to and from school daily, studying English literature. While she loved and admired her mother, it was her aunt, her mother's sister, Dr. Lillian Powers, who was the most powerful inspiration in Lillian's life. Dr. Powers was one of the first women to enter the field of psychoanalysis and studied with Freud in Germany.

In 1900, Lillian graduated with a bachelor's degree in English literature and was the first female commencement speaker at UC Berkeley. Her original intention had been to earn a master's degree at Columbia University with the well-known writer and educator Brander Matthews, but he did not allow women to study with him or attend any of his lectures. Edward Thorndike accepted women students, so she took two of his courses instead. This was her first real exposure to psychology as a discipline. She threw herself wholeheartedly into her studies, often skipping meals until she grew thin and weak. When cold weather set in, she became very ill and had to return home to California.

In 1902, Lillian finally finished her master's degree in literature at her alma mater, the University of California, Berkeley. She planned a trip abroad to celebrate her accomplishments before beginning her doctoral studies. She spent a few weeks in Boston prior to leaving for Europe, visiting with her traveling companion and friend, Minnie Bunker, and her family. This is where Lillian met her future husband, Minnie's cousin Frank. Bunker Gilbreth Frank was young, very handsome, gregarious, and extroverted. He was also the wealthy owner of a construction company. He took the women sightseeing in his new car. Lillian, then twenty-five, and Frank who was thirty-five, immediately fell in love. Upon her return from Europe, Frank was waiting with flowers.

Three weeks after Lillian was back at home in Oakland, Frank visited her there, met her family, and proposed to her. They were married on October 19, 1904. During their honeymoon trip, Frank requested of her a list of qualifications she was bringing to their "partnership." However formal and rigid that might sound, the two made it work splendidly for years to come. Although Frank never went to college, he was very intelligent, self-taught in many areas, and almost obsessed with efficiency in the workplace. They began their life together, working on various projects. Lillian, it seems, was as passionate about the subject as he was. They immersed themselves in scientific management principles. She was an engineering apprentice and a full partner in the construction business. They worked well together.

Lillian soon noticed that the engineers were addressing their technical issues scientifically, but they seemed unaware of human psychological aspects. She firmly believed that scientific management systems were extremely neglectful of the needs of the individuals in a work setting. She understood the need for a scientific model to identify the most beneficial motions to improve efficiency. Lillian also wanted to identify the best motions, thus providing the most beneficial results for the workers who were using them. It was an interesting concept and difficult to sell. She argued that psychology had an equally important place in their studies. So, while Frank was studying the motions of the employees, Lillian was observing and analyzing how the employee felt, along with what level of dedication they had toward their work.

Lillian's Ph.D. studies were almost complete in California. The dissertation she presented for her Ph.D. in California was cutting-edge. It was read and viewed as very positive and worthwhile. Unfortunately, at the very last minute, her Ph.D. was not conferred by the Academic Senate of the University. She had not met the requirement of her final year in residence because she had not wanted to leave her family. She attempted to publish her dissertation, but initially, no one would print it because it was considered avant-garde, way ahead of its time, and of little interest to most readers. Lillian opted to publish the dissertation in small installments in engineering periodicals. Eventually, it was published in its entirety as a book in 1914. The Psychology of Management became one of the most influential texts on the subject. However, the publisher was still reluctant to have a woman named as the author, so Lillian was identified ambiguously as L.M. Gilbreth. Lillian Gilbreth developed a reputation as a key player in industrial management in her own right, independent of her husband.

In 1910, Frank and Lillian moved to Providence, Rhode Island, and started their family. Lillian convinced Frank to give up the construction business in 1912 so they could devote all their time and expertise to management consulting. The couple opened their new business, Gilbreth, Inc., where Lillian felt they could better test their ideas and perfect strategies. Their work included implementing very novel ideas for the time, such as rest periods, employee suggestion boxes, and process charts. Based on employee perspectives, they redesigned jobs to focus more on workers' welfare, than on other popular practices where workers were perceived in relation to profit. Together, they developed strategies to employ workers with various challenges, enabling them to become productive community members.

The theme that underlaid all of Lillian's work, was that a human component must be included. Lillian and Frank shared the goal of applying what they knew of scientific management to many areas outside of the industry. For example, the two employed their knowledge to aid in developing more efficient surgical techniques and methods of rehabilitating people with physical handicaps. Frank and Lillian also started workshops out of their home, in which they trained managers to use their techniques. In addition, they worked as consultants, traveling to businesses to observe and improve business operations. In 1913, they started the Summer School of Scientific Management, teaching their method. Attendees were academic and industry professionals from around the world. In 1914, Frank went to Germany to visit industrial plants, teach, and consult.

When World War I broke out, wounded soldiers filled the hospitals. Frank helped to improve surgical procedures and introduced motion-picture photography to help educate surgeons. He was the first to propose that a surgical nurse serve as a "caddy" (his term), to hand instruments to the surgeon, as called for. Frank became quite knowledgeable in the care and rehabilitation of the injured. He also devised the standard techniques used by armies around the world to teach recruits how to rapidly disassemble and reassemble their weapons even when blindfolded or in total darkness. These innovations have probably helped save millions of lives.

Frank recognized Lillian's keen insight into human behavior and her strong empathy for individuals, as well as her genuine interest in psychology. He supported her while she completed her studies. Her second dissertation was, "The Elimination of Waste," earning her a Ph.D. in Industrial Psychology from Brown University in 1915. Lillian had chosen Brown when the couple moved to the East coast because it was nearby, and it was one of the first universities to acknowledge scientific management as a legitimate course of study and profession. Her focus, in part, concerned the application of psychology and scientific management to the work of classroom teachers; her thesis asserted that scientific management proponents must consider the happiness and perspectives of the workers. Hers was the first degree granted at Brown in industrial psychology. Lillian graduated with four little Gilbreths in tow.

Frank and Lillian were a perfect team, and both became very passionate about finding the "one best way" to perform any task with the goal of increasing efficiency and productivity in the workplace. Frank was totally focused on the technical aspects of worker efficiency and Lillian on the human aspects of time management. Not only did they apply their concepts and methods to their business, but also to their own household. Over a seventeen-year period, the Gilbreths had twelve children. Two of those children, Frank Jr., and Ernestine, co-authored two books, *Cheaper by the Dozen* and *Belles on Their*

Toes, which contained accounts of family life in the Gilbreth household, and were sometimes very humorous. Both books were later made into movies.

Frank, it seems, was a bit of a fanatic about household efficiency. He developed methods, sometimes rather unorthodox, of making the household run as smoothly as possible. He applied scientific management principles and methods to his own family. The Gilbreth home almost seemed like a "mini-industry." There is one amusing story of daily life in the Gilbreth household that illustrates this perfectly: "Frank took moving pictures of his sons and daughters at work to analyze their motions and thus find ways to help them perform a task (for example, washing dishes) more quickly and efficiently. He set up process and work charts in the bathroom so that even the youngest children could record each morning when they had brushed their teeth, taken a bath, combed their hair, and made their beds. In the evening, each child noted his weight and plotted it on a graph before filling out the process charts to indicate whether he had brushed his teeth, washed his face, and done his homework. A family council met once a week to create a budget (a separate purchasing committee handled shopping duties) and to assign regular chores. To earn extra money, the children submitted sealed bids for special jobs such as painting a fence or removing a tree stump (the lowest bidder won the contract). A utility committee monitored water and electricity usage and fined those who left a light on or a faucet running. A designated gift-buyer kept track of birthdays and other special occasions and bought presents."

Lillian was among the first to recognize and document the effects of stress and fatigue on time management. Unfortunately, her findings were not embraced during her lifetime, though Lillian's extensive research was instrumental in setting the course of modern management. Lillian recognized what motivated workers; direct incentives such as money and indirect incentives such as job satisfaction. Together, she and Frank helped to set a standard for jobs, incentive wage plans, and job simplifications. When the United States entered the war, Frank enlisted in the Engineers Officers Reserve Corps. However, he could not serve as he had developed heart problems and the family moved to Nantucket, Massachusetts, for his recovery.

In 1924, back at home in Montclair, New Jersey, Frank had a heart attack and died on June 14. He was only fifty-six years old. Frank's death left Lillian with the sole responsibility of providing for her family of twelve children and managing the consulting business. She knew the business well enough. After all, she and Frank had always been equal partners. Lillian assumed she could continue to run the business by herself. She soon discovered that many companies were unwilling to do business with a woman and either canceled or refused to renew contracts with Lillian alone. One can only imagine what this brilliant and capable woman must have felt, suffering the loss of her beloved husband, the respect she had earned, and her livelihood, all at the same time.

Lillian moved her family to California, where she hosted workshops in her home to train managers. In this way, she could be with the children as well as continue her career and business. It seemed like a good idea that would work, but it too proved difficult, she was a woman and people did not believe she was credible! With time and patience, the workshops took off and became successful. Her reputation grew, and she was invited to consult with some prominent businesses.

Lillian was then involved with the marketing research on sanitary napkins for Johnson & Johnson in 1926. Her training as a psychologist, and her image as a mother and a modern career woman, helped the company build consumer trust. Lillian also consulted for Macy's department store in New York City, where she worked as a salesperson to get a clear picture of what the working conditions were really like. The store was so thrilled with her success at improving productivity, they asked Lillian to train one of their executives to implement her techniques.

Lillian went on to work for General Electric, where she interviewed over 4,000 women and collected data on simple household chores, such as collecting garbage or washing dishes. Then she used that data to design the proper height for sinks, stoves, and other kitchen appliances.

Lillian patented many appliances that made work in the kitchen easier. She also authored two books: *The Homemaker and Her Job,* in 1927 and *Living with Our Children,* in 1928. Her focus was the belief that, "homes should be happy places in which individuals can achieve fulfillment and a degree of freedom," and she felt strongly that, "wives and mothers are entitled to share in this freedom and fulfillment, but this happy situation can be attained only if the responsibilities of the home are shared and efficiently handled." In other words, every housewife and mother must be an effective and efficient manager.

Lillian's reputation was flourishing and soon she received so many requests for her services that she taught a course at colleges and universities, such as Bryn Mawr, Rutgers, and Purdue Universities. In 1935, Lillian Gilbreth attained a full professorship at Purdue. (Lillian continued to teach at Purdue until her retirement at age seventy).

Lillian's government work began because of her longtime friendship with Lou Henry Hoover and her husband Herbert Hoover, both of whom she had known previously in California. When Hoover was president, he asked Lillian to join the Emergency Committee for Unemployment during the Great Depression. Lillian accepted and created her own very successful nationwide program, "Share the Work," which she designed and promoted to create new jobs. Lillian presided over the Women's Branch of the Engineers for Hoover's presidential campaign. At the request of Lou Hoover, she joined the Girl Scouts as a consultant in 1929, later becoming a member of the board of directors. Lillian remained active in the organization for over twenty years.

During World War II, Lillian worked as a consultant to the government in war plants and on military bases. She also worked at the Arma Plant, which handled Navy contracts in Brooklyn, New York. In 1948, Lillian taught at Newark College of Engineering in New Jersey. From 1953 to 1954 she taught in Formosa, and then in 1955 she taught at the University of Wisconsin.

Lillian's work as a consultant continued, and she applied her principles more and more to American homemakers, hoping to save housewives time and energy. Who could understand the life of a housewife better than Lillian, who had twelve children and a brilliant career? She was very successful in both designing and implementing innovative and valuable inventions, such as shelves on refrigerator doors, wastewater hoses for washing machines, and the foot pedal lid on trash cans. She even designed an electric mixer.

In the 1940s, the *California Monthly* described Lillian as "a genius in the art of living," because of her extraordinary ability to successfully combine a brilliant career and family. As one of the first working female engineers holding a Ph.D., she was credited as the first true industrial/organizational psychologist. Lillian Gilbreth was vital and active in psychology and management until she was ninety years old. Throughout her illustrious career, she received many awards, including twenty-two honorary degrees from schools such as Princeton University, Brown University, and the University of Michigan. She served as a visiting professor at Stanford, Harvard, Yale, and the Massachusetts Institute of Technology, to name a few.

In 1921, Lillian Gilbreth was the first female member admitted to the Society of Industrial Engineers.

In 1924, Lillian was inducted into the American Society of Mechanical Engineers and was chair of their Management Division's meeting on the psychology of management.

Lillian was a Fellow of the American Psychological Association.

Lillian received the first Gilbreth Medal for distinguished contributions to management from the Society of Industrial Engineers.

In 1944, Lillian and Frank were awarded the Gantt Gold Medal from the American Society of Mechanical Engineers and the American Management Association.

In 1952, J.W. McKenney declared Lillian Gilbreth "The World's Greatest Woman Engineer," because of her "impact on management, her innovations in industrial design, her methodological contributions to time and motion studies, her humanization of management principles, and her role in integrating the principles of science and management."

In 1966, Lillian was the first woman to receive the Hoover Medal for distinguished public service by an engineer.

In 1984, the United States Postal Service issued a postage stamp in Lillian's honor.

Lillian and her husband Frank have a permanent exhibit in The Smithsonian National Museum of American History and her portrait hangs in the National Portrait Gallery.

Suggestions for further reading:

Lillian Gilbreth: Redefining Domesticity (Lives of American Women) by Julie Des Jardins

Making Time: Lillian Moller Gilbreth — A Life Beyond "Cheaper by the Dozen" by Jane Lancaster

As I Remember: An Autobiography by Lillian Gilbreth

Mary Ann Ball Bickerdyke

"I watched the dreadful combat until the
clouds hid all from view..."

Mary Ann Ball was born in Knox County, Ohio, on July 19, 1817, to Hiram and Annie Cassady Ball. Her father was a farmer. Her mother died when she was just seventeen months old. Hiram, now a grieving and overwhelmed widower, sent Mary Ann to live with her elderly grandparents, who farmed in Richland County. Upon their deaths, she went to live with her uncle, Henry Rogers, on his farm in Hamilton County, Ohio. Mary Ann had a very limited basic education, and her childhood was difficult, being shuffled from relative to relative.

At age sixteen, Mary Ann moved to Oberlin, Ohio, where some accounts say she worked in the home of a professor as a domestic. She attended Oberlin College, one of the few institutions of higher education open to a woman in the United States, though she did not graduate. Mary Ann received training as a nurse in Cincinnati, where she worked assisting doctors during the cholera epidemics of 1837 and 1849. (These horrible epidemics took thousands of lives, including Harriet Beecher Stowe's infant son in 1849.)

In April 1847, Mary Ann married Robert Bickerdyke, a widower with three children. He was a sign painter and musician. Both Mary Ann and Robert were ardent abolition activists, transporting escaping slaves by wagon to safety. In 1849, Mary Ann gave birth to their first child, John, who sadly only lived for a few minutes. Later, the couple had two sons, James and Hiram, and a daughter, Martha. Martha died when she was only two years old.

In 1860, after only twelve of marriage, Robert died, leaving Mary Ann to support the remaining family. After Robert's death, the family moved to Galesburg, Illinois, where Mary Ann was a member of the Congregational Church. She opened a practice in "botanic" and alternative medicines using herbs and plants, which she studied in Cincinnati prior to her marriage. Mary Ann was now relying on those skills for her livelihood.

One Sunday in 1861, during a church service at the Galesburg Congregational Church, the Rev. Dr. Edward Beecher, brother of Harriet Beecher Stowe, spoke about the horrible neglect of the Illinois volunteers who had become sick with typhoid and dysentery at a Union Army camp in nearby Cairo. Mary Ann hadn't heard of their plight before. Rev. Beecher read a letter to the congregation that was sent by Dr. Woodward, who was a surgeon with the 22nd Illinois Infantry and a friend of Mary Ann's. He wrote persuasively, begging for help. The letter described the conditions at the camp, and it so moved the congregation that they donated $500 to the cause. Mary Ann organized the relief fund, procured supplies, and took them to the camp for disbursement. No one else would go. She left her children, now ages twelve and thirteen, in the care of a neighbor. Her stepchildren were grown and gone from the home at this point. Mary Ann headed to Cairo, becoming a nurse in the Union Army. She was forty-four years old.

Upon Mary Ann's arrival at the camp, she was horrified to discover that the situation was even more squalid than Dr. Woodward had described. Conditions were foul, crowded, and unsanitary, and there was little food. Mary Ann set to work immediately without waiting for permission from anyone, which became her way.

Mary Ann began cleaning, feeding, and nursing the sick men, launching a four-year career helping the sick and wounded of the Civil War, both at the front lines and behind them. She had barrels cut in half for the men to bathe in and clothes were sent by the congregation back home. Huge kettles were set up over a fire where soups and porridge simmered, and tea and coffee brewed. Loaves of bread were baked in brick ovens; eggs, milk, and fresh vegetables were secured from local farmers. Healthy meals were prepared for the injured and recovering soldiers. They deserved the best, and Mary Ann was determined to see they got it!

It was during this time that Mary Ann met Mary Livermore, an associate member of the United States Sanitary Commission. The Commission had recognized Mary Ann's organizational genius and fortitude, which included floating a herd of cows down the Mississippi and Ohio Rivers to provide hospitalized soldiers with fresh milk and beef. Mary Ann was appointed as a field agent for the Northwestern branch of the Sanitary Commission, earning $50 a month. Until this time, she had been working for the army with no official appointment, rank, remuneration, or authority - although, authority always seemed to be *her* trademark.

Mary Livermore also helped Mary Ann find care for her two sons while she was in the field. Mary Ann used her salary to settle her sons in a boarding house in Beloit, Wisconsin. They were vociferous in their complaints about leaving the neighbor's care and moving to Beloit, but Mary Ann was confident that they were old enough to be away from her and would receive good care in their new situation, which they did.

Mary Ann searched daily for the wounded and when darkness fell, she listened at the edges of the battlefields for the groans of wounded men that were overlooked. When she heard them, she went out herself through rain and storms and depending on the time of year, sometimes icy conditions, with lanterns and stretchers to bring them back to the field hospital for care. When bandages ran low, she tore up any of her own clothing that would serve the need. Holding the hands of wounded and dying men, Mary Ann sang songs of home and heaven to them so they would not feel alone and afraid. She referred to them affectionately as her "boys." The grateful men referred to her as "Mother" Bickerdyke.

Once Mary Ann had the camp at Cairo squared away, she knew her work had just begun. Her next stop was Fort Donelson, where she joined a field hospital, working side by side with Mary J. Safford, who had just left a teaching position in Illinois to care for the sick and injured. Mary Safford was a nurse, physician, educator, and humanitarian, who was often called the "Cairo Angel." It was here at Fort Donelson, Mary Ann witnessed her first actual battle, resulting in her determination to work even harder for the sick and wounded soldiers.

Mary Ann realized very critical laundry services were lacking in field hospitals. Packing up all the soiled clothes and linens, she added disinfectants to the load and sent the bundle on a steamer to Pittsburg Landing to be laundered. Along with that bundle, was a request for washing machines, portable kettles, and mangles. When a surgeon questioned Mary Ann's authority to take some action or other, she replied, "on the authority of Lord God Almighty, have you anything that outranks that?" Mary Ann hired escaped and former slaves to provide laundry services for her field hospitals. Those hospitals were basic canvas tents, old storehouses, and makeshift sheds, often hidden in the woods.

From Fort Donelson, Mary Ann went to Gayoso Block Hospital, in Memphis, Tennessee. One morning, she discovered that the assistant surgeon had been on a drunken spree the night before, causing him to sleep late. He had neglected to make out the special diet list for his ward. As a result, his seriously wounded patients had no breakfast and were faint with hunger. Confronting the negligent surgeon, Mary Ann reprimanded him in harsh terms. According to many sources, the doctor laughed off her scolding and asked what the problem was. "Matter enough you miserable scoundrel!" She responded, "Here these men, any one of them worth a thousand of you, are suffered to starve and die because you want to be off upon a drunk! Pull off your shoulder straps, for you shall not stay in the army a week longer." Three days later, the errant doctor was discharged. Bickerdyke authority!

At each site, Mary Ann fought passionately for the welfare of her soldiers. Understanding the importance of nutritious food, she acquired cows and hens to provide fresh food at the hospital. One day after running errands, Mary Ann returned to find the medical doctor on duty had dismissed all her help. She was furious and went to the man in charge, Brigadier General Stephen Augustus Hurlbut. The Brigadier General gave her written authority to reinstate and retain all her employees until he himself revoked the order. He also ordered Presidents Island reserved for exclusive use by Mary Ann and her "crew" for the pasture and care of the cows and chickens she had procured.

Mary Ann had opposition because she was a woman Her "take charge" demeanor most likely rankled many a man. News of this reached General Grant. Consequently, he appointed Mary Ann Matron of the hospital. This gave her official status when she previously had none. Mary Ann handled the care of 900 patients, 400 of whom were Native American. Here, as with her other hospitals, she employed as many escaped and freed slaves as possible. From battle site to battle site, Mary Ann was there. She was "Mother" to them all. The nurse wearing a plain, often soiled gray calico uniform; changing dressings, serving a hot meal, offering a cool drink, comforting, cooling a feverish brow, heating bricks for a cold bed, brewing coffee, assisting with amputations, and quieting the fears of sick and injured "boys."

Mary Ann eventually became chief of nursing under the command of General Ulysses S. Grant and served at the battle of Vicksburg. Unafraid of stepping on anyone's toes, she occasionally and blatantly ignored military procedures when she felt it necessary. Mary Ann was often brutal to officers and physicians she deemed lax or neglectful. She had no sympathy when reporting dereliction of duty, particularly drunkenness. On one occasion, Mary Ann even ordered a staff member, who had appropriated garments meant for the wounded men, to strip! She was tenacious and had several of the wayward staff dismissed.

Mary Ann kept her position as chief of nursing through the favor and influence of Grant, Sherman, and a few others who recognized the great value of her services. Otherwise, she might have been sent packing, too. She was masterful at upsetting the status quo, but only because she wanted the best for her soldiers. Her knowledge of botanical medicine stressed the necessity of clean water, wet compresses, herbal teas, healthy soup, steam inhalation for ailments of the lung, fresh fruits, and vegetables, and, foremost, cleanliness. This led her to be very intolerant of careless practice. Mary Ann's methods were credited with saving more lives than the inept physicians working in those field hospitals under filthy conditions. Over 400,000 of the estimated 620,000 Civil War deaths were not from battle wounds but from diseases caused by unsanitary conditions.

When staff complained about Mary Ann, and they did, General William T. Sherman reportedly threw up his hands and exclaimed, "She outranks me. I can't do a thing in the world." She was called "Brigadier Commanding Hospitals." It was well-known and understood that she was "one of the best generals." Mary Ann earned the title "Cyclone in Calico" because of her indomitable spirit, high energy, sharp focus, and disregard for regulations when it was to the detriment of her "boys". Doctors and officers often bristled and balked at her take-charge stance, but she continued her mission in a no-nonsense, pragmatic manner.

Mary Ann followed the western armies, and both Sherman and Grant always sanctioned her efforts, providing her with supplies she couldn't get without their sway. Friends of high rank who appreciated her were invaluable. Grant moved his troops down the Mississippi, and Mary Ann went with them, setting up hospitals where needed. Grant gave her a pass for free transportation anywhere in his command.

On October 14, 1863, when Mary Ann reported to Chattanooga, Tennessee, she witnessed the battle of Lookout Mountain, named "the battle above the clouds." "I watched the dreadful combat until the clouds hid all from view." Mary Ann set up a field hospital for the Fifteenth Army Corps, which fought the Battle of Missionary Ridge. For four weeks, Mary Ann was the only female attendant at this site. Some of her work during this period was collecting personal items of the soldiers who died in battle and returning them to families, or at least to the soldiers' homes. A grim job, but an important one. There were many things collected, including photos of loved ones and letters that would never find the mail pouch. Even many years after her death, former Governor Yates of Kansas noted that "she bound up the wounds of the afflicted and when she did so, she administered a soothing balm to the lacerated hearts at home."

In 1864, Eliza Porter joined Mary Ann, and the two worked together for about nine months in Chattanooga, Tennessee, and Huntsville, Alabama. Eliza was a schoolteacher from Chicago, the first public school teacher to arrive at Fort Dearborn. She left teaching to assist the Sanitary Commission in setting up hospitals. Mary Ann later accompanied the forces of General William Tecumseh Sherman on their march through Georgia to the sea. She provided frequent medical examinations and transport for men who could no longer walk. Sherman was especially fond of this colorful nurse volunteer who followed the western armies. It is said she was the only woman he would allow in his camp.

In 1865, when this brutal war ended, "Mother" had built over 300 hospitals and aided the wounded on nineteen battlefields, including Shiloh and Sherman's March to the Sea. Mary Ann was so treasured by the men that they always cheered when she appeared. General Sherman even invited her to lead the Grand Review of the Armies down Pennsylvania Avenue in Washington, D.C., and arranged a seat in the reviewing stands for her. While Mary Ann marched at the head of an entire army corps in the parade, she refused the seat in the stand, saying she preferred to set up a latrine and a refreshment center along the parade route. Mary Ann was once again a civilian.

In 1866, Mary Ann worked for a while at the Home for the Friendless in Chicago, Illinois. Then Colonel Charles Hammond, president of the Chicago, Burlington, and Quincy Railroad funded her to help fifty Veterans and their families move to Salina, Kansas as homesteaders. After months of relentless persuasion, Jan Hodge, wife of a Presbyterian Minister, and Mary A. Livermore, her old friend from the Sanitary Commission, convinced Mary Ann to take part in a lecture tour to raise funds and supplies for the injured, disabled, and returning soldiers. Mary Ann much preferred caring for soldiers to fundraising and was often very curt with her audiences when appealing for their financial support. Mary Ann had been at the front! There was no way she could convey in mere words the terrible horror and the great pain caused by the war--or the enormous need that existed now. For example, when in Milwaukee, Wisconsin, her "thank you" to the Chamber of Commerce for a donation sounded brusque and perhaps a bit less than sincere, "I am glad you are going to give $1,200 dollars a month for the poor fellows in the hospitals; for it's no more than you ought to do, and it isn't half as much as the soldiers in the hospital have given you." Mary Ann continued comparing the Chamber's monetary contribution to the limbs and lives of the soldiers in the field and secured a $10,000 donation from Jonathan Burr, a banker, to help the veterans get land, tools, and supplies. She had not lost her touch for gaining support for the soldiers, her "boys."

Mary Ann was voted the first president of Lyon Women's Relief Corps of Oakland. In 1870 she went to New York for a while at the request of her friend, Mary Jane Safford, and the Protestant Board of City Missions who had begged her help in cleaning up some of the worst slums. While Mary Ann was in

New York, her sons had begun to farmland she had claimed for them in Great Bend, Kansas. They asked her to come home to the farm and live with them, a request Mary Ann eventually honored.

Mary Ann's work was not over yet. When locusts destroyed the crops in the Kansas settlement during the summer of 1874, Mary Ann came to the rescue again. She made many trips and gave hundreds of speeches asking for help for the farmers, and returned with 200 carloads of grain, food, and clothing that helped sustain them. With the help of General Sherman, Mary Ann ran a hotel that was known as the Salina Dining Hall, but the name was changed to Bickerdyke House. True to her character, she just could not charge those who were hungry or in need. This resulted in a loss of backing and consequently the hotel. After losing the hotel, Mary Ann worked at the San Francisco Mint and the Salvation Army in California.

On May 9, 1886, a bill was passed by congress granting "Mother" Bickerdyke a special pension of $25 a month. Representative Long of Massachusetts introduced the bill. Generals Grant, Sherman, and

Pope all testified on her behalf, supporting it. Mary Ann Bickerdyke taught the world a very important lesson, it only takes one person to bring about massive change. Despite many and insurmountable obstacles, Mary Ann elevated the value and importance of the nursing profession and always fought for what was right.

Mary Ann's sons forgave her for sending them away during the war years. In 1887, she went to live with her son James in Kansas, where he was the principal of the high school. In 1895, the Kansas Historical Society honored Mary Ann Bickerdyke for her contributions to preserving the state's past. The state of Kansas initiated a statewide celebration proclaiming July 9 "Mother" Bickerdyke Day. Eighty-year-old Mary Ann enjoyed it tremendously!

Suggestions for further reading:

Cyclone in Calico: The Story of Mary Ann Bickerdyke by Nina Brown Baker

Civil War Nurse, Mary Ann Bickerdyke by Adele De Leeuw

Mary Fields

"My name is Mary Fields...People call me
Stagecoach Mary"

Mary Fields was born a plantation slave in Hickman
County, Tennessee, in 1832 or 1833. Like many
other enslaved people, neither the exact date nor the

place is known for certain. Some accounts say she was born in the home of Judge Edmund Dunne and his wife, Josephine, who had five children. Although Mary was literate, she left no written history.

Slaves made up twenty-five percent of the population of Tennessee and they were the unwilling backbone of the state's agricultural production. Tennessee was home to many of the largest slaveholding plantations. This included President Andrew Jackson's Heritage Plantation in Nashville, where One hundred fifty Black men, women, and children were enslaved on his 1,000-acre plantation.

By all accounts, the Dunne's were a devout Catholic family, who were kind and caring. Mary formed an unlikely friendship with one of their daughters, Sarah Dunne. They were as different as night and day. Sarah had a fair complexion, blond hair, and blue eyes and was a descendant of a wealthy Irish family. Mary, on the other hand, was a dark-skinned slave, with black hair and dark eyes. Sarah was frail and delicate, while Mary was strong and sturdy. Sarah was refined and patient, and Mary was rough and quick-tempered. The Dunne's offered Mary the same opportunities for education as Sarah. She learned to read and write as Sarah did, a rarity. Unusual though it was, Mary and Sarah, or "Dolly" as Sarah was called, were about the same age and had formed a deep and lasting friendship.

Mary's mother, Susanna Dunne, was the house slave and the owner's favorite cook. Mary was always in the house with her mother, rather than in the field. This is how Mary and Dolly became lifelong friends. Mary's father, Buck, was a field slave. When Mary was born, Susanna wanted her daughter to have a last name, so they used "Fields" because Buck was a field slave. What a tragic commentary on the lives of slaves who lost their "personhood." Slaves lost everything!

Slavery was outlawed in 1865, though Mary stayed close to the family who had owned her because of her deep friendship with Dolly. In 1881, Dolly became an Ursuline nun and moved to the little town of Cascade in the far western corner of Montana, between Helena and Great Falls. Her task was to set up a school for women and girls of the Blackfeet Indian Tribe.

Mary moved to Mississippi, where she worked for a while as a chambermaid on the steamboat, The Robert E. Lee. She was on board during the famous boat race with the Natchez in 1870. Mary was a great storyteller and enjoyed relating her experience of watching the men toss anything they could find – barrels of resin, sides of ham, bacon, and even furniture – into the boiler while other men sat on the relief valves to boost the steam pressure and their speed. "It was so hot up in the cabins that the passengers were forced to take to the decks," she said, according to an article in a local newspaper in 1914. "It was expected that the boilers would burst." She was fearless though and viewed these escapades as a splendid adventure.

Mary and Dolly stayed in touch, writing long letters to one another during this time. Eventually, Mary joined Dolly at the Ursuline convent when Dolly was in the novitiate in Toledo, Ohio. When Dolly was posted to the outpost in Montana, Mary's propensity for adventure propelled her further into the world of travel and exploration.

Then in 1885, Dolly, now known as Mother Amadeus, became quite ill and sent a letter asking Mary to come to Cascade. Mother Amadeus' illness was serious, and she wanted the comfort and nursing of her dear friend and childhood companion. Mary nursed Mother Amadeus with great love and care until she regained her health. Mary saw things that needed doing at the convent and school and just jumped right in.

Mary soon had a team of willing men laboring alongside her making repairs to the ramshackle establishment. Mary cut wood and hauled supplies from the rail station back to the mission, grew vegetables, and raised and cared for four hundred chickens. She was highly valued. It was not long before she became forewoman at St. Peter's Mission. Mary dug post holes and helped with the construction of the new schoolhouse and a chapel. She accomplished this with little more than her bare hands, a pocket full of nails, and a carpenter's level. Mary alone handled the team of horses that drew the wagon, which brought visitors and critical supplies to the convent. She had a genuine talent for horses and insisted on working with them herself regardless of the weather.

One dark and stormy night, when Mary was traveling home from getting food and supplies in town, a pack of wolves spooked the horses, and the wagon overturned. She stood guard, gun at the ready, using the wagon as cover throughout the night to protect the food and other vital supplies for the convent. The nuns depended on these supplies to survive, and she must protect her Dolly. When the sun came up the next morning, she tracked down the horses, muscled the wagon back upright, put the supplies back in place, and headed for the convent. Mary saved everything except a keg of molasses that had cracked on impact. The bishop made her pay for that molasses out of her own pocket.

The rural west suited Mary. Being a slave had conditioned her to a life of hard work. Mary was about six feet tall and weighed over two hundred pounds. If her size didn't draw attention, her style certainly did! She wore comfortable trousers under her skirt and apron for warmth, a wool cap, and sturdy boots. That apron was very handy for hiding her five-shot Smith & Wesson .38 revolver, and she was not afraid to use it. Mary was a formidable figure. It was said that she was a match for any two men in Montana. Mary had a standing bet that she could knock a man out with one punch, and she never lost a dime to anyone foolish enough to take her up on that bet. The locals did not know what to make of Mary. Some Natives called her "White Crow" because "she acts like a white woman but has black skin." Mary was the first Black woman to settle in this part of the country.

One day, when Mary was away running errands, a few of the nuns did some of Mary's chores while she was gone. They did laundry with no problems, and then they burned a small pile of trash. This is when it turned from a helping hand to a disaster. The fire ignited some loose cartridges that were inexplicably laying on the ground, leaving Sister Gertrude slightly wounded over one eye when they went off. They were most grateful when Mary returned home.

The chaplain at nearby Fort Keough, Father Landesmith, visited St. Peter's in 1887. Mary captivated him with her storytelling, relating her battle with a skunk. Said skunk had been invading her chicken coop and killed over sixty of her baby chicks. Mary was fighting mad. She shot the skunk and dragged it more than a mile to show off her trophy, to both the sisters and visiting chaplain. They were impressed, but also stunned, asking her how in heaven's name she could accomplish this and not get sprayed. She explained she took great care to make a frontal assault.

When the sisters moved from the primitive log cabins into a new stone building, Mary personally hauled the few possessions of her beloved Dolly, using a wheelbarrow. She continued her work at the Mission for almost ten years and would have spent the rest of her life there had it been allowed. But it was not to be.

Stories of Mary's escapades mounted. There was a gun duel, in wild west fashion, but few details are available. Tales of fistfights, which Mary won, were more readily available. During a trip to a neighboring ranch, Mary got into a heated debate over some harnesses with the ranch foreman. She used a small rock to emphasize her point of view, leaving a permanent dent in his skull. On another day, one of the "hired hands" lodged a complaint that Mary was earning $2 per month more than he was and he was a man! She earned $9 per month, and he earned only $7. It was unthinkable! The disgruntled man faced her and asked just who she thought she was, that she was worth so much money, and she, just an uppity colored woman?! To make critical matters worse, he voiced these same grievances at the saloon where she was a regular, and then he took his grievance to the bishop! This set Mary's blood to boiling, once again.

At the very next opportunity, Mary and the hired hand engaged in a full shootout behind the nunnery next to the sheep shed. Bullets flew in every direction until both guns were empty. Neither hit the other, but one bullet Mary shot bounced off the stone wall of the convent, hitting the despicable man in the left buttock, thus ruining his new trousers for which he had paid $1.85. Some of the other bullets passed through the laundry drying on the line, ventilating a pair of trousers and two white shirts belonging to Bishop Brondel, the first Catholic Bishop in Montana. He had just had them shipped from Boston only the week before. It was never clear just what the bishops' clothes were doing on the convent clothesline, but that was quite enough for the bishop. Between the ruination of his new clothes, the gun battle, and other stories that had reached him, his patience had run out. Bishop Brondel fired Mary on the spot and gave the injured man a raise.

Mary traveled with Mother Amadeus to Helena to plead her case but to no avail. The powers that be had already decided that she must leave St. Peters. Mother Amadeus was devastated, yet unable to go against the wishes of her bishop. She did the next best thing by securing a mail route for Mary between Cascade Center and the convent. That way, she could still see her dear friend, and Mary would have employment. Somehow, Mother Amadeus found her friend a wagon along with a mule named Moses for the new job. Mary Fields became only the second woman in the country to manage a mail route and the first African American. The first known appointment of a woman was Sarah Black in April 1845. Mary was grateful for the job and worked at it for eight years.

For Mary's "interview," she was told to hitch a team of six horses to the coach as quickly as possible. Her competition was a handful of hardened, grizzled old cowboys. The sixty-year-old Mary blew them away; she hitched the horses and had time to run over to the saloon, grab a beer, come back, and smoke a cigar. All while waiting for the others to finish up. Hired!

Mary broke all the barriers to delivering mail in the Wild West. This was not a job for the weak or faint of heart. It carried tremendous risks and required long and arduous days on horseback, often in hostile territories. It was still an untamed and lawless land. There was a saying at the time that "the horse and rider should perish before the mail pouch did." Successful delivery, it seems, was valued more than life itself. Once again, Mary Fields rose to the occasion.

Her nineteen-mile route was a ride between Cascade and St. Peters, which gave her the opportunity to return to the people and place she loved, the place from which she was exiled. It was during this time that the lively mail woman became known as "Stagecoach Mary." One historian noted that when she rode into town, she made her presence known to all. One man wrote: "With a jug of whiskey by her foot, a pistol packed under her apron, and a shotgun by her side, (she) was ready to take on any aggressor. The shotgun Mary toted was one of the most feared guns. It could cut a man in two at short range, and Mary would not hesitate to do so."

Mary never missed a day of work and she forged ahead regardless of the weather. When the snow was too deep for Moses to make it, she strapped on her snowshoes and hauled the heavy sacks on her shoulders. Mary also placed the highest value on delivering that mail. Everyone knew they could count on Mary. She had rough edges for sure, and the sisters attempted to smooth some of them by inviting her to practice the Catholic faith and attend services. This didn't work well, as Mary preferred the rougher company of the men who worked at the convent or in town.

Mary worked hard, played hard, swore mightily, could drink any man under the table, played cards, smoked nasty, homemade cigars, fought with her formidable bare hands, loved swapping stories with the men, could argue politics with anyone, was a crack shot – and she had a heart of gold. Mary couldn't find this kind of satisfaction in a church.

During one of her earlier mail runs to the convent, Mary was hurt badly when the team of horses she was driving spooked, and she lost control. It was not clear why she was driving a team of horses and not her steady mule, but she knew if she had her mule, Moses, this never would have happened. Arriving at the convent, she was feeling very guilty for having let the horses get away from her. Some sisters used this as an opportunity, once again, to encourage Mary to practice her faith and attend mass with them. She surprised everyone by agreeing to attend the following day. Several of them stayed up most of the night to fashion a beautiful blue challis dress and a long white veil for Mary to wear on this momentous occasion. What a picture that must have been!

Mary loved baseball and adopted the local Cascade team as her own. The team loved her as well and invited her to all their games, home or away. For each game, she prepared little buttonhole flowers from her own garden for each of the players to wear. She reserved the larger bouquets for any man hitting a home run. Anyone speaking ill of that team within her earshot could expect a bouquet of knuckles in his face! Mary also loved children and often babysat within her community. She charged $1.50 per hour and would then turn around and spend most of it buying treats for the children.

Mary met a little boy from Montana who was visiting family friends in Cascade. When Mary asked him his name, he replied, "Gary Cooper." In 1959, Mr. Cooper remembered her fondly when he wrote an article for *Ebony* magazine, "Mary could whip any two men in the territory and had a fondness for hard liquor that was matched only by her capacity to put it away. Born a slave somewhere in Tennessee, Mary lived to become one of the freest souls ever to draw a breath, or a .38."

The famous cowboy artist, Charlie Russell, lived in Cascade for a short period and was captivated by Mary Fields. In 1897, Mr. Russell depicted her in a pen and ink work called "A Quiet Day in Cascade." The drawing portrayed Mary carrying a basket of eggs and being knocked down by an errant hog, causing her to spill the fragile contents.

Sometimes Mary took in laundry for the men in town to make a little extra money. By proclamation of the mayor, D.W. "Bill" Munroe, she was the only woman of reputable character in Cascade allowed to drink at the local bar. She enjoyed this privilege and could put away her fair share, but never drank to excess.

One day, Mary was in town enjoying a cold beer with the boys when she saw a man outside who owed her $2. She jumped up and marched to the door. A hush fell over the bar. She walked right up to that man, and with one swift jab to the jaw, laid him on the ground, rendering him unconscious, and knocking a tooth out. As Mary returned to the bar, she brushed her hands off and said, "consider that debt paid in full!" She was seventy-two. Upon regaining consciousness, he realized that the tooth he lost had been giving him great trouble anyway. He was most grateful, rather than upset. Often, the men learned respect for Mary the hard way. *The Great Falls Examiner*, the local paper, once declared that "Mary broke more noses than any other person in central Montana… any man challenging her was a hardheaded fool."

Mary retired from the U.S. Postal Service, yet she still needed a source of income. She opened a couple of restaurants, but soon they went broke because she extended credit or didn't charge anyone in need. Deciding that perhaps the restaurant business was not for her, Mary opened a laundry service that was more successful. In 1903, her longtime friend and mentor, "Dolly," went to Alaska to establish another mission. It devastated Mary. Mother Angelina, who succeeded Mother Amadeus at St. Peters' was kind to her, but it was little comfort after such a sorrowful separation from her Dolly. Mary's heart was broken.

Mary Fields was now a well-known figure. She was loved and respected by all in Cascade, as well as surrounding areas. The local hotel always welcomed her and in 1910, when R.B. Glover leased the New Cascade Hotel from Kirk Huntley, there was a clause in the lease stipulating that Mary would always, and with no question, have free meals for the rest of her life. The town declared her birthday a formal holiday. Schools and businesses closed for the day! This eighty-plus-year-old woman used to laugh uproariously since the exact date of her birth was unknown. Mary simply chose two different days, and everyone celebrated twice.

In 1912, Mary's home burned to the ground. The ashes were hardly cool when the entire town showed up to rebuild for her. Businesses and schools closed, and it was all hands on deck at the building site.

People from many walks of life gave whatever they could–temporary housing, clothing, food, and funds. Mary was respected and well-loved for sure.

The entire town attended Mary's funeral. People came from far and wide. It was reportedly the largest funeral in Cascade ever. Telling this story does not glorify brawling, violence of any kind, drinking, or smoking. Kept in the frontier's context in the 1800s, it celebrates the life of a wom'n who was brave, dedicated, loyal, loving, hardworking, and strong. Mary Fields was dauntless, with no fear of man or beast...a legend in her own time.

Suggestions for further reading:

Deliverance Mary Fields, First African American Woman Star Route Mail Carrier in the United States: A Montana History by Miantae Metcalf McConnell

"Stagecoach" Mary Fields by Julie McDonald

Mary Fields by James Franks

Mary Fields aka Stagecoach Mary by Erich Hicks

Films in which Mary Fields is represented:

In the documentary South by Northwest, "Homesteaders" (1976), Mary Fields is played by Esther Rolle.

In the TV movie "The Cherokee Kid" (1996), Mary Fields is played by Dawnn Lewis.

In the TV movie "Hannah's Law" (2012), Mary Fields is played by Kimberly Elise.

In the short Western, "They Die by Dawn" (2013), Mary Fields is played by Erykah Badu.

Martha Maria "Mattie" Hughes Cannon

"Somehow, I know that women who stay home all the time have the most unpleasant homes there are. You give me a woman who thinks about something besides cook stoves and wash tubs and baby flannels, and I'll show you, nine times out of ten, a successful mother."

Martha Maria Hughes was born near Llandudno, Wales, on July 1, 1857, the second of three daughters born to Peter and Elizabeth Evans Hughes. She was called "Mattie." The family had converted to the Church of Jesus Christ of Latter-day Saints (LDS) and immigrated to the United States on March 30, 1860.

In 1861, they left New York City and began the arduous journey across the country to Utah. It took them three months in a covered wagon to reach their destination, Salt Lake Valley. Before their arrival on September 3, 1861, Mattie's sister, Annie Lloyd Hughes, died and was buried along the trail in an unmarked grave. She was twenty-one months old. Three days later, the remaining family arrived in Salt Lake City. After their arrival, on September 17, Peter Hughes died. Elizabeth, at twenty-eight years old, had become a widow with two young daughters.

Since the Mormons practice a form of socialism, where no member of the faith community is left unprotected, Elizabeth's plight of being a young widow with children was not as dire as it might have been.

Many women in this community operated their own businesses and assumed responsibility for other young women who were intelligent and motivated. These qualities were recognized in young Mattie and the women supported her scholastic endeavors.

A year later, Elizabeth met James Patten Paul, who was a widower. They were married and had five additional children. Mattie and her stepfather were close. She loved him very much and he loved her. At different intervals in her life, Mattie went by the names of both Paul and Hughes. She had always dreamed of becoming a medical doctor and shared that dream with her stepfather. James Paul was an enormous influence in Mattie's life and encouraged her to always be herself, and follow her dream of becoming a doctor, no matter how out of reach it may seem. "Make it happen," he would say.

When she was fourteen, Mattie taught school. Later she became a typesetter at the *Women's Exponent*, a women-run newspaper in Salt Lake City, that was published by Emmaline B. Wells. In 1870, the paper celebrated when women in the Utah Territory won the vote. This was only weeks after the Wyoming Territory had set the precedent. Emmeline was an American journalist, editor, poet, women's rights advocate, and diarist. Emmeline served as the fifth Relief Society General President of The Church of Jesus Christ of Latter-day Saints from 1910 until her death.

Mattie was an impressionable teenager who grew up accustomed to the unusual grit and status of Mormon pioneer women. Her entire community supported her when she enrolled at the University of Deseret, graduating in 1875 with a degree in chemistry. This was extraordinary for a woman during this time in history. In 1878, Mattie enrolled in medical school at the University of Michigan and earned her M.D. in 1880. Mattie was twenty-three years old and living her dream. She practiced medicine for a short period in Algonac, Michigan. In 1882, Mattie earned a B.S. in Pharmacy from the

Auxiliary School of Medicine of the University of Pennsylvania, where she was the only woman in a class of seventy-five students.

Mattie cut her hair short to save time and wore men's boots to keep her feet dry. Women's fashion dictated undue discomfort and fuss. She was focused on her studies and would have none of it. Mattie also earned a diploma from the National School of Elocution and Oratory, as she believed it was necessary to improve her public speaking skills. Mattie, who always had a seriousness of purpose, worked hard at everything she did. She was often found washing dishes, working as a chambermaid, or doing secretarial work to help finance her studies.

In 1882 Mattie returned to Salt Lake City, where she served as the resident physician for four years. She also established the first training school for nurses at the Deseret Hospital. It was here that she met Mr. Angus Cannon, who was the superintendent of the hospital. Mattie married Angus on October 6, 1884. She became the fourth wife of his six plural wives and bore him three children. He was twenty-three years her senior.

In April 1886, under great pressure from the federal government, Mattie Cannon left Utah with her infant daughter Elizabeth Rachel. Angus had been arrested on polygamy charges. Mattie wanted to avoid testifying against her husband, as well as others in the community. The legislation was passed and was being enforced regarding polygamy. The authorities gathered information by seizing the records at her obstetrical practice, making it risky for her to remain in Salt Lake City. She wrote in 1885: "Hence I am considered an important witness, and if it can be proven that these children have actually come into this world, their fathers will be sent to jail for five years... To me, it is a serious matter to be the cause of sending to jail a father upon whom a lot of little children are dependent, whether those children were begotten by the same or different mothers, the fact remains they all have little mouths that must be fed."

To get out of town and avoid arrest herself, Mattie hid under a blanket in the back of a hay wagon with Elizabeth. She spent two years in exile in England, then Switzerland, before returning to Michigan. "I would rather be a stranger in a strange land and be able to hold my head up among my fellow beings," she reflected late in her exile, "than to be a sneaking captive at home." When she returned to Michigan, Mattie learned Angus had taken a fifth wife. The relationship became a little strained after this news, but Mattie just wanted to be home.

Mattie once again took up her medical practice, teaching and working for women's rights, specifically suffrage. She was a featured speaker at the Columbian Expo in Chicago at the World's Fair in 1893 as a part of the delegation of women from Utah. Mattie traveled to Washington D.C. to speak to a Congressional Committee in favor of granting women the right to vote in the United States. She was adamant that public service and education were vitally important for women. In her own words: "Somehow, I know that women who stay home all the time have the most unpleasant homes there are. You give me a woman who thinks about something besides cook stoves and wash tubs and baby flannels, and I'll show you, nine times out of ten, a successful mother."

In 1896, in a much-publicized election, Mattie ran as one of the five Democrats "at large" for a Senate seat. This was also the year that Utah women gained the right to vote by passing a suffrage clause in the new state constitution. Mattie spent a grand total of $35 on her campaign. Among the five Republican candidates running for office was the suffrage activist Emmeline B. Wells, her former employer, and her husband, Angus! Martha Hughes Cannon was easily elected on November 3, 1896, becoming the first woman ever to be elected to that office in the United States, and served two terms in the Senate. The election caused a little discord and a temporary rift in her marriage, but apparently, they reconciled. Mattie gave birth to her third child in 1899 while holding office. Local papers noted that a leading Mormon polygamist was defeated by his fourth wife. Another editorialized that Angus Munn Cannon was deserving of his readers' votes, while another countered with "Mrs. Mattie Hughes Cannon, his wife, is the better man of the two. Send Mrs. Cannon to the State and let Mr. Cannon, as a Republican, remain at home to manage the home industry."

During her two terms, Mattie targeted issues of public health, raising funds for speech and hearing-impaired students, establishing a state board of health, and laws regulating working conditions for women and girls, "An Act to Protect the Health of Women and Girl Employees." When her legislative term was up, she served as a member of the Utah Board of Health and as a member of the board of the Utah State School for the Deaf and Blind. In her later years, Mattie divided her time between Salt Lake City and Los Angeles. Angus Cannon died on June 7, 1915, in Utah. By the early 1920s, Mattie settled near her son in California, where she worked for the Graves Clinic.

In 1986, the Martha Hughes Cannon Health Building was dedicated in Mattie's honor.

In 1996, an eight-foot bronze statue of Mattie Cannon was installed in the Utah Capitol Rotunda, 100 years after her election as a state senator. The statue was reinstalled on the capitol ground following the renovation of the building.

Suggestions for further reading:

Pioneer, Polygamist, Politician: The Life of Dr. Martha Hughes Cannon by Mari Grana

Letters from Exile: The Correspondence of Martha Hughes Cannon and Angus M. Cannon, 1886-1888 by John Sillito and Constance L. Lieber

Ellen "Nellie" Cashman

"When I saw something that needed doing, I did it."

Ellen "Nellie" Cashman was born in 1845 and baptized on October 15, 1845, which was probably not long after her birth. Typical of Irish Catholic families, her baptismal date was more important than her birth date. Nellie's parents were Patrick and Frances (Cronin) O'Kissane, though the name was later anglicized to Cashman. The family lived in the farming village of Midleton, a few miles from Cobh (then Queensland), in County Cork in the South of Ireland. Nellie had a younger sister, Fanny.

These were the years of the Potato Famine, and people were starving. This was a very hard time in Ireland. The worst year of this period was 1847, known as "Black '47." During the Great Hunger, about one million people died and more than a million fled, causing the country's population to fall by twenty to twenty-five percent. Between 1841 and 1851 some areas fell as much as sixty-seven percent. The Cashman family felt the pinch even more severely when Patrick died sometime around 1850.

Nellie's mother, hoping to make a better life for herself and her two daughters, immigrated to America. Nellie was scared but also excited to leave Ireland. While they were waiting to board the ship, she encountered a young fiddler, Timothy O'Flannagan, who assured her "Don't you worry, little one, it will all come right," and it did.

The journey was long and arduous aboard the cramped ship, with many people sick. Some died. Nellie was a mere five years old when they landed in America. They first settled in Boston, where there were tens of thousands of Irish. Nellie's mother, Fanny, thought it would be a safe place, but soon discovered that despite the number of Irish, there was huge and often violent prejudice against them. She knew that this was not going to be a good place to raise her daughters. As soon as she had set aside sufficient funds, Fanny resettled in Washington, D.C., hoping life would be a little better.

When they reached Washington, D.C., Nellie was about ten years old. She was an ambitious young girl, very determined, and wanted to help her mother with the great financial burden of supporting the family. Dressed in boy's clothing, short pants, a tweed jacket, and a pork-pie hat, Nellie soon secured a job as a bellhop in a grand hotel. She was a good worker, and the bosses liked her because she did her work and kept her mouth shut. After a short while, Nellie received a promotion to elevator operator. While doing this job, she overheard people's conversations, many of which were about the Civil War. The year was 1861.

One of Nellie's passengers, who was a large man, dressed fashionably, with eyeglasses and whiskers, smiled at her. He and his companions smelled of leather, wool, and cigar smoke. He was animated and spoke loudly about the war. Quietly and unnoticed, Nellie listened to all of it. She knew that this man was someone important. He was a frequent passenger. One afternoon, leaving the elevator car, he stopped, patted Nellie on the head, and complimented "him" on "his" work. He said "he" had a wonderful spirit and should go west, where there was an unlimited possibility for "him." They "chatted" on a few other occasions. The older man had taken a liking to this elevator operator. Nellie later learned this big man was indeed important. He was General Ulysses S. Grant, who worked with President Lincoln during the war, and of course, later became the 18th President of the United States.

Nellie and her mother worked hard and saved, denying themselves all but the smallest luxuries. The goal of a better life in the west was foremost in their minds. When the small family had enough saved, they took Grant's advice and began the journey west. They sailed the Atlantic, crossed the Isthmus of Panama on donkeys, and sailed the rest of the way to San Francisco, where there was a large Irish Community. Nellie was now twenty years old.

Nellie saw a need for a good restaurant and opened one. She advertised that it was clean, honest, and had good food. For a few years, it made a handsome profit. Her sister Fanny, Nellie's youthful confidant and best friend was now in her late teens and approaching twenty herself. Fanny met a handsome Irish bootmaker by the name of Tom Cunningham. They fell in love, married, and began a family of their own.

With Fanny married and gone, Nellie became enamored with the gold and silver strikes in Nevada. She and her mother traveled up to this remote and rugged area. What a dauntless pair they were, working side by side. Nellie, always the adventurer, was soon hired as a cook in various Nevada mining camps, including the Virginia City and Pioche mines. She earned the nicknames Pioche Nellie and Irish Nellie.

These were some of the roughest mining camps in the west. Nellie was always quick to make friends with the miners, often feeding them and providing lodging when they had no money or other resources. *The Daily Record* named Miss N. Cashman, a proprietress who offered "good board at low rates" and noted, "The Table will be supplied with the best to be had in the Market."

Nellie worked and saved and in 1872, opened her own boarding house and restaurant at Panaca Flat, Nevada. She was now twenty-two years old. Mother and daughter soon earned a reputation for being honest, clean, and having wonderful food, in a town that hosted seventy-two saloons and thirty-two brothels.

When she heard of a gold strike in British Columbia, restlessness overtook Nellie. Traveling to South Africa was also on her mind and she couldn't decide which she wanted to do more, so she flipped a coin.

In the end, she joined a group of 200 miners going to the Cassiar District of British Columbia, at Dease Lake in the Telegraph District. There, Nellie opened another boarding house and restaurant, resulting in the same success she had previously enjoyed. Despite feeding boys who had no money, she did a glorious business and turned a handsome profit. While she was living in this remote area, she began to study facts about mining and learned much from the miners themselves at her boarding house and saloon. Nellie grubstaked miners and sold them Cunningham Boots, which were about the best made, and all miners needed boots. She could now send money home to Tom and Fanny.

Nellie did well enough at Dease Lake to finance a trip further north after the mining season ended. In the hard winter of 1874-75, she heard that miners who had elected to winter over up north were starving and suffering from scurvy. She hired six men, gathered pack animals, and took 15,000 pounds of supplies and provisions, including limes to combat the scurvy. They traveled for seventy-seven days in snow sometimes ten feet deep. Nellie nursed 100 sick miners back to health, most likely saving their lives. While she was there, she also taught them some basic nutrition.

Conditions in these mountains were so hazardous at the time, even the Canadian Army refused to mount a rescue. When they heard about Nellie's expedition, they were in a panic. The commander sent his troops to find her and escort her back to safety. However, when they located her, Nellie was in her tent, drinking tea, snuggled under a couple of wool blankets, and reading a book, with her little stove blazing away. She offered the men tea, and thanked them for their efforts, but refused to return without the stranded miners. She stood barely five feet tall and weighed less than 100 pounds, but when Nellie put her mind to something, nothing was going to deter her!

The Cassiar strike played out and Nellie headed for San Francisco to nurse her elderly and frail mother. Nellie still had mining fever. When her mother died, she packed up once again and set out for the silver fields of Arizona. She arrived in Tucson in 1879, opening The Delmonico Restaurant, the first business in town owned by a woman. It was wildly successful, despite, or perhaps because of, her habit of caring for and feeding hungry, sick, or hapless miners. Nellie again studied mining, ore, and geology. She was bright, a fast learner, and was becoming an expert in mining.

In 1880, Nellie sold the Delmonico and headed to the San Pedro Valley and the new silver boomtown of Tombstone. The Earp brothers had just arrived in town a few weeks ahead of Nellie. She bought and ran a boot and shoe store. The following is an ad from the *Tombstone Daily Nugget*, dated April 1, 1880: "Miss Nellie Cashman, of the famous Delmonico restaurant, in Tucson, has opened a gent's furnishings good store in Tombstone, on Allen Street, adjoining Ward's market. She will keep a large supply of furnishing goods, both for the ladies and gentlemen, including boots and shoes, and as Nellie was never outdone in any business she has undertaken, her success in our midst is double sure."

Feeding hungry miners seemed to be a role that fit Nellie, and she opened yet another restaurant. This one was the Russ House, named after her original restaurant in San Francisco. She served fifty-cent meals and advertised that "there are no cockroaches in my kitchen and the floors are clean." A popular legend claims that a diner once made a disparaging remark about Nellie's cooking. Doc Holiday was dining there that evening and heard the remark. He jumped up, and drew his pistol, asking the customer to repeat what he had said. The man said, "Best I ever ate."

Tombstone was still a bit wild and wooly. Gunfire was often heard echoing through the streets. On a particularly loud afternoon, an old, grizzled, prospector, clothes in tatters with a faded sweat-stained hat atop his head, asked Nellie if she was afraid of the gunfire. She responded that she wasn't unless they came closer to her place. Having just finished one of Nellie's hearty meals, he sighed and said, "probly all Tombstone needs to be the garden spot of the world, is good people like you and water." Nellie smiled, and said, "Well stranger, I reckon that's all Hades needs too."

When Tom Cunningham died of tuberculosis at age thirty-nine on February 20, 1881, Nellie brought her sister Fanny, who was very weak and in ill health herself, and her five children, to Tombstone to live with her. Fanny helped Nellie out in whatever way she could. Being a devout Catholic, Nellie was very concerned that there was no church in town. She had forged a strong friendship with Wyatt Earp, the marshal of her town. She approached him with her concern, now heightened because Fanny and her children were there. They needed a church! His reply was something like, "well, well, Miss Nellie, my wee Colleen, if you need a church, you shall have one." He closed his saloon, The Crystal Palace, for a half day on Sunday for Nellie to hold church services. Wyatt Earp also helped her raise money. It didn't take long before the Sacred Heart Church was built.

During her years in Tombstone, Nellie gained a reputation as an angel of mercy. She was a prominent and influential citizen, well-loved and well-connected. Nellie was very involved in raising money for the Red Cross, the Miner's Hospital, and amateur theatrical performances that were staged locally. She also took up collections for injured men or men who had fallen on hard times. Nellie found the members of the red-light district sympathetic and charitable to her causes. She often relied on their generosity to help others in need. When a miner died in an accident or of illness, there was no fund for his widow or children. Nellie would go up and down the streets with her hat turned upside down, collecting for the family. The source of the donation never bothered her. Most days, she finished up with a full hat. "Whether the money comes from an upstanding citizen, or a member of the outlaw faction makes no difference to me," she said. "The money doesn't know the difference either. What matters is what it is used for, and I see to it that in one way or another, it helps humanity."

Nellie earned various nicknames, including, "Angel of Mercy," "Saint of the Sourdough," "Miner's Angel," and "Angel of Tombstone." Her biographer, Don Chaput, said of her, "She is as pretty as a Victorian cameo, and when necessary, tougher than two-penny nails." He captured Nellie in those few words. Years later, Major John P. Clum, former owner of a prominent Arizona newspaper, who was duly impressed with Nellie, wrote: "Her frank manner, her self-reliant spirit, and her emphatic and fascinating Celtic brogue impressed me very much, and indicated that she was a woman of strong character and marked individuality."

In December 1883, Nellie was serving as an officer of her church and heard the impromptu confessions of two of the five men who were to be hanged for the Bisbee Massacre, which took place on December 8, 1883. Five outlaw cowboys robbed the Bisbee General Store, killing four people and maiming two others. It was common knowledge that Bisbee didn't have a bank. Consequently, the payroll for the Copper Queen Mine was delivered to the general store a few days before the actual payday.

Four of the five men responsible for that crime were convicted on March 28, 1884. They were the first criminals to be legally hanged in Tombstone, which was then the county seat. This was a highly charged and emotional event. Law enforcement and townspeople wanted to make a spectacle of the executions.

A local carpenter built a grandstand adjoining the hanging gallows and planned to sell tickets. Nellie was outraged. She believed that no execution should ever be celebrated, and convinced Sheriff Ward to set a curfew on the day of the hangings to prevent crowds from gathering. Before dawn, on the day of the execution, Nellie looked into the stern faces of a formidable group of strong and resolute men. "You lead us to that grandstand, and we'll do the wrecking," was their firm response as they picked up their tools. Nellie nodded and issued a curt command, "Come on men," and she led the way to the Court House. When they arrived, Nellie picked up a sledgehammer, and with a well-directed blow, shattered the first supporting beam. The following hour was very busy and saw the complete destruction of the grandstand.

The executions took place as scheduled, but privately and out of sight of a jeering public. When Nellie learned that medical school students planned to exhume the bodies of the convicts to use for study, she enlisted two prospectors to stand watch over the Boot Hill Cemetery for ten days, ensuring that none of the bodies were disturbed. None were. The mastermind of the robbery was tried separately and sentenced to life in prison. Bisbee citizens were unhappy with this lenient sentence and organized a lynch mob, extracting him from jail, and hanging him on February 22, 1884. Evidently, the crowds were still hungry for a spectacle.

Nellie's commitment to justice and the town continued into the following year. A group of miners attempted to lynch Mr. E. B. Gage, the wealthy owner of the Grand Central Mine, during a vicious labor dispute at his mine. Nellie sprang into action. Borrowing a wagon, and with an ax and other tools, she dismantled the gallows that were prepared. In the dark of night, Nellie drove a borrowed buggy slowly and seemingly invisibly, right through the rioting miners, spiriting Mr. Gage out of town. She left him at the train station in Benson so he could flee by rail. She said, "it all came right." There is speculation that this story is more urban legend than fact. It seems her nephew, Michael Cunningham, a prominent banker in Cochise County, was also a superb storyteller and a big fan of his Aunt Nellie. The actual story may never be known.

Nellie made many mining claims. Some she kept and others she sold, but Nellie always seemed to know where the strike would be, and she almost always profited. Nellie had a sense, the "Luck of the Irish" if you will, to go along with a keen knowledge of geology and business. The Harquahala rush saw her prosper, but when that subsided, Nellie was restless. She traveled throughout the west and maybe even to Africa. It had called to her before.

In the summer of 1883, after word of a big strike, Nellie organized a group of twenty-one prospectors and headed for Baja, California. They traveled for six days by train and ship, then they had to continue the journey on foot. The group had not counted on or planned for the blistering heat of the barren desert. Their search for gold, they now realized, was futile, and they needed to focus on survival. Their water was running low, and the group was suffering from dehydration and heat exhaustion. They were in a dire situation. Nellie was the strongest of the group and had a firm faith that her angel would guide her. She assured the remaining twenty that all would be well again. Nellie headed out in search of water and found a Catholic Mission tucked away behind the sagebrush and cactus.

A kindly, elderly Padre helped Nellie load up water and supplies for the weary and half-dead group of would-be prospectors. A day later, she returned to the group in the company of several Mexicans, leading pack mules with food and goatskins filled with water. While the trip was disastrous and nearly fatal, Nellie was recognized and praised for her pluck, resourcefulness, and strength. She was ultimately responsible for saving them all. On the return trip, she booked passage for the group on a small Mexican craft. During the voyage, they noticed the captain was drunk and could not master the vessel. Nor could he stop drinking. He was a danger to them all. Some men immobilized him and tied him up. Nellie then locked him up, took control of the boat, and with a little help, got them safely to the port of Guaymas. When released in port, the now sober skipper accused Nellie of piracy on the high seas. This was a very serious charge. She held her own with the Mexican authorities with a little help from her traveling companions and her enormous charm. Nellie was soon home in Tombstone. Some say this oft-told tale was embellished. Who knows?

During one of her mining expeditions, she may have found love. It was reported by a local paper, the *Phoenix Daily Herald*, in February 1889, "Mike

Sullivan, one of the Bonanza mine owners at Har Camp, left there yesterday in the company of Miss Nellie Cashman, on their way to the nearest station where a minister could be obtained, in order to be made man and wife." However, a marriage never happened. Nellie left the camp around this time, and Mike apparently headed back east, not to be heard from again. Perhaps they fell out of love on the way to the preacher.

Nellie was quite an expert in ore and mining by now. Her travels took her to various sites in Arizona; Globe, Nogales, Prescott, Jerome, Harquahala, and Yuma. She also explored Kingston, New Mexico, and Sonora, Mexico. There are substantial gaps in detailed records during this time. It was not long after Nellie's nearly disastrous trip to Baja that she learned that her beloved sister Fanny had also died of tuberculosis in 1886. This left Nellie with the responsibility of raising Fanny's five children.

Nellie sold Russ House and left Tombstone with Fanny's children in tow. In the company of her nieces and nephews, who were then teenagers, Nellie prospected in Arizona, Idaho, and Montana. In

1895, she even made a quick trip to Juneau, Alaska. Nellie always returned to Tombstone to wait for news of the next big strike.

Michael Cunningham, Nellie's eldest nephew, remembered this time, "We were always on the move, looking for gold and silver." Despite their roaming, all five children received great support from their Aunt Nellie, and the best education available, (sometimes as borders, in various Catholic schools). All five children grew into adulthood as successful, productive citizens. Mr. Cunningham became one of the most influential citizens in Cochise County. He was the president of the Bank of Bisbee and the Bank of Lowell. He said all of this was because of, "the care, counsel, and encouragement of his Aunt Nell."

In 1896, there was a gold strike in the Klondike. It was said that a gold nugget the size of a dime was found in a small tributary of the Klondike River, called Rabbit Creek, later to be renamed the world-famous Bonanza Creek. Because of extreme winter weather and the remoteness of the area, it took almost a year before the news spread. That led to a stampede of thousands of prospectors, not only from the United States but from all over the world. When Nellie heard about the strike, she began making plans to go to the Klondike. News of her forthcoming trip made headlines in local newspapers. *The Tombstone Prospector* wrote Nellie Cashman was "the only woman mining expert in the United States." When asked about her planned trip, Nellie replied, "Going to Alaska! Well, I should say I am."

On January 1, 1896, the *Mohave County Miner* wrote: "Miss Nellie Cashman left last Wednesday for the Klondike... Miss Cashman is the best-known woman in Arizona, having made two or three fortunes in mining speculations in the early days, and has watched the rise and fall of more mining camps than any other woman in the West. The land of the eternal glaciers has no terrors for her, and the good wishes of her many friends in Arizona go with her. Success to the honest, fearless little woman." When asked by a reporter from the Daily Colonist what she might wear for such an expedition, Nellie replied, "I dress... in many respects, as a man does... long heavy trousers and rubber boots. Of course, when associating with strangers, I wear a long rubber coat. Skirts are out of the question up north, as many women will find out before they reach the gold fields."

Nellie had planned to meet her nephew, Michael, and a male friend who would accompany her on the journey. Inexplicably, neither showed up at the designated meeting place in San Francisco, so she resolutely set off alone on the arduous journey to Alaska. The indomitable Nellie headed north up along the Pacific coast to Victoria, and then on to Skagway. From there, she ventured onto Chilkoot Trail, heading toward Chilkoot Pass. This mountain route had several paths with meandering and turbulent rivers that were nearly impossible to cross. The prospectors endured hazardous and extremely harsh conditions on their ascent to the pass, climbing the steep and treacherous 15,000 steps called the 'golden stairs,' which had been cut into the deep snow and ice. They trudged their way through thirty miles of raging storms with sleet and rain. Some lost their lives in frequent avalanches.

Once they reached the summit, the Northwest Mounted Police Station wisely mandated, and strictly enforced, the regulation that anyone entering British Columbia must have with them a full year's supply of food. The trail was too steep for animals. The prospectors had to carry their own provisions, making many trips over the pass. This might have taken from several weeks to months before they could proceed. Nellie was now a middle-aged woman, but a very determined one. She trudged on, making it to Lake Bennett where they continued the 500 miles down the perilous Yukon River in hand-hewn boats, through dangerous rapids and canyons to Dawson City. They went through the Five Finger Rapids, the White Horse Rapids, and all the others. Nellie commented on this leg of the journey, "Believe me, it's some journey all right to go through those rapids. I never want to travel any faster than I did there."

They estimated that only 30,000 of the 100,000 would-be prospectors, actually completed the trip. Nellie finally reached Dawson in April 1898. She was fifty-four years old. The city was bustling and filled with about 40,000 people. She settled there for the next seven years, staking mining claims, and running several restaurants and stores. It was in Dawson that Nellie made one of her richest claims. The No.19, below Dawson, made her over $100,000, which she then invested in other claims. "I spent every red cent of it buying other claims and prospecting the country. I went out with my dog team, or on snowshoes, all over that district looking for rich claims." In 1901, only one percent of miners in the Yukon were women. Though very mild-mannered, compassionate, and extremely generous, Nellie was a veritable force to be reckoned with when protecting a claim from poachers. She took no grief from anyone. Let a poacher try to worm his way into her claim... he would be sorry, very, very sorry.

Many of the miners spent evenings in a local saloon. Most likely they were lonely. Nellie converted a portion of one of her stores into a quieter, alternative place for miners to chat while drinking a free cup of coffee. It was commonly referred to as "The Prospectors Haven of Retreat." John Clum, the former owner of the *Daily Arizona Citizen*, who had also made the trek to Dawson, and had been a great admirer of Nellie Cashman, wrote: "She was generous to a fault, always helping some worthy, but hard-up miners. She always said, 'If a young fellow was broke and hungry, I would give him a meal for nothing.'"

Nellie's generosity often left her penniless, but the miners never forgot her kindness to them. Alex MacDonald and Jim McNamee, who had made their fortunes twice over in the Klondike, would always, "supply her with sufficient gold dust to put her back on easy street." She would inevitably turn around and give it to another charitable cause. Nellie loved her miners and lived her life showing that. The miners loved her too! John Clum also noted that while Nellie preferred to live among the men, she was a devout Catholic and lived her faith. She "maintained an unimpeachable reputation, and her character and conduct commanded the universal respect and admiration of every community in which she lived."

In 1902, Felix Pedro, a self-taught Italian Immigrant, found gold in Fairbanks, Alaska. Early in 1903, prospectors from the Klondike rushed to the district hoping to hit it big. Many became discouraged and returned to the Yukon, after discovering the ground in a deep freeze. By 1904, Dawson was in decline, and serious mining was happening in Fairbanks because the ground was rich and the field very large. Nellie heard about this and her "prospecting bug" bit again. After leaving Dawson, and arriving in Fairbanks, the first thing Nellie did was open a store, look for a good claim, and begin fundraising for the Episcopalian St. Matthews Hospital. Her fundraising efforts were initially staking herself in some of the many poker games that were being played in some of the well-off mining camps. Nellie also toured the camps on a dog sled, soliciting donations for the Hospital. She would tell them, "Okay boys, this is for the hospital. If you've got money to throw away at poker, you can give it to them hardworking Christian women that's takin' care of the sick."

In 1907, Nellie set out on her last expedition to a remote region several hundred miles further north, the Koyukuk District. Koyukuk is in the southern foothills of what is now called the Brooks Mountain Range. During Nellie Cashman's time, shallow draft steamboats were used to reach the district—a journey of over 400 miles. Then in smaller boats to Bettles Trading Post, and an additional eight miles up the Middle Fork of the Koyukuk to Nolan Creek.

Nellie settled in a camp called Coldfoot, sixty miles north of the Arctic Circle, working various claims around Nolan Creek.

During Nellie's time in the Koyukuk District, there was the promise of a big load, but the ground was frozen solid, with the gold about 100 feet down. Because of the remoteness and inaccessibility of the district, transportation costs were very high, but to be productive, the ground needed to be thawed. It was just not in Nellie to give up, so she purchased expensive steam boilers and piping for herself and the others at camp. The boilers allowed productive mining until the 1920s.

Nellie formed the Midnight Sun Mining Company and sold shares to help cover the costs of the outfit. The miners in the Koyukuk District were old and conservative. They appeared to thrive on whiskey, but that did not seem to interfere with their mining. The Episcopal Bishop, Rowe, wrote of these old, conservative, whiskey-drinking individuals, [they are] "The type which has pioneered the way into this country for their fellow men, and who have the true spirit of the North. I do not believe that you will find a finer lot of men in any community than those Koyukuk miners." Nellie did well in those years and frequently left the area during the deep of winter, to visit friends and family, especially her favorite nephew, Michael, back in Arizona. She always returned to her cabin in Koyukuk, and she remained in Alaska for almost twenty years.

In 1921, Nellie visited California where she declared boldly to the authorities that she would like to be appointed the U.S. Deputy Marshall for the Koyukuk mining district. Apparently, they did not take her seriously, as it never came to pass.

Nellie was still spry and quite capable of mushing her dogs hundreds of miles on these trips in and out of the Koyukuk District. *The Associated Press* documented a dog sled trip she made from Nolan to Anchorage in 1922. In December 1923, after completing a seventeen-day, 350-mile trip from Nolan Creek to Nenana by herself, newspapers all over Alaska carried the story of this intrepid, indestructible, seventy-eight-year-old Irish "lass," a woman miner by the name of Nellie Cashman. Some say that she was truly a woman who matched the mountains. In her letter to her nephew, Michael Cunningham, confirming her safe arrival in Nenana, she reported, "The sled only turned over once. I had a little roll in the snow."

When a reporter from the *Arizona Star* interviewed her late in her life, Nellie was asked about marriage. She had never married. The reporter asked her why. Her reply was priceless! "Why child, I haven't had time for marriage! Men are such a nuisance now, aren't they? They are just boys grown up. I have nursed them, embalmed them, fed, and scolded them, acted as mother confessor, and fought my own with them and you have to treat them just like boys." The *Arizona State Miner* described her as "one of Arizona's most picturesque pioneers." In his tribute to her, John Clum wrote, (she was) "a noblewoman, whose energetic, courageous, self-sacrificing life was an inspiration on a wide frontier during half a century."

Nellie Cashman was immortalized on the twenty-nine-cent stamp issued by the United States Postal Service on October 18, 1994.

In 2006, the Alaska Mining Hall of Fame honored Nellie.

In 2007, Nellie was inducted into the National Cowgirl Museum and Hall of Fame in Fort Worth, Texas.

In June 2014, a monument was erected in Nellie's honor near her home in County Cork, Ireland.

Jack Crawford, Robert W. Service, Joaquim Miller, and Jack London all wrote about Nellie.

Suggestions for further reading:

Gold Rush Queen: The Extraordinary Life of Nellie Cashman by Thora Kerr Illing

Nellie Cashman: Frontier Angel by Ronald Wayne Fischer

Nellie Cashman: Prospector and Trailblazer by Suzann Ledbetter

Nellie Cashman and the North American Mining Frontier (Great West and Indian Series, V. 63) by Don Chaput

Toughnut Angel: The Tale of a Real-Life Adventuress of the Old West by Jane Carlile

Sarah Emma Evelyn Edmonds Seelye

"I am naturally fond of adventure, a little ambitious, and a good deal romantic - but patriotism was the true secret of my success."

Sarah Emma Evelyn Edmonds was born in December 1841, in Magaguadavic, New Brunswick, Canada. She was the youngest of five children growing up on a farm, along with her sisters. Their father was hoping for a son to help him with the chores on the farm. He was very disappointed when another girl arrived. He showed his resentment by abusing Sarah as she grew up. She described her family as overprotective, making her feel "sheltered but enslaved," and characterized her father as the "stern master of ceremonies." Sarah received little education as a child but enjoyed reading very much. It was a pleasant escape for her. Fanny Campbell, the Female Pirate Captain by Maturin Murray Ballou, inspired her. The main character, Campbell, maintained a male persona during the American Revolution and had many bold and amazing adventures on a pirate ship.

In 1850, when she was fifteen, Sarah ran away from her abusive father, an arranged marriage, and her home. Her mother assisted her in the escape, maybe because she herself married very young and understood Sarah's plight. She first changed her name to Emma Edmonds and got a job as a salesgirl in a millinery shop. The shop was a place of peace for her for a couple of years. Sarah, now called Emma, lived and worked in the little town of Moncton, but was always afraid her father would find her, and he did. Once again, she escaped.

Sarah immigrated to the United States to find permanent safety and peace of mind. This time, she changed more than her name. She adopted a male persona and became "Frank Thompson." This was inspired by Ballou's book, her childhood favorite. This male disguise allowed her to eat, travel and find employment with more ease, and she hoped to avoid being tracked down again by her father. Sarah maintained her identity as "Frank Thompson" while she traveled and after arriving and settling in Hartford, Connecticut. It wasn't long before she found work as an itinerant bible salesman.

Now, quite established as "Frank Thompson," Sarah made her way west. By 1861, she was living in Flint, Michigan. In her memoir, Sarah recalls she was sitting in a train station, a very successful bible "salesman" when she heard the news that the Civil War had broken out. It upset her and jolted her awake. She knew she must act. "I was aroused from my reverie by a voice in the street crying 'New York Herald – Fall Of Fort Sumter – President's Proclamation – Call For Seventy-Five Thousand Men!' This announcement startled me, while my imagination portrayed the coming struggle in all its fearful magnitude... It is true, I was not an American, I was not obliged to stay here during this terrible strife, I could return to my native land where my parents would welcome me to the home of my childhood, and my brothers and sisters would rejoice at my coming. But these were not the thoughts which occupied my mind. It was not my intention, or desire, to seek my own personal ease and comfort while so much sorrow and distress filled the land. But the significant question to be decided was what can I do? What part am I to act in this great drama? I could not decide for myself, so I carried this question to the Throne of Grace (a reference to the Bible, Proverbs) and found a satisfactory answer there."

It was just a month later, on May 25, 1861, that "Frank Thompson" enlisted in the United States Army. After training in Washington, D.C., they sent

263

"Private Thompson" south to work in McClellan's campaign in Virginia, as a male field nurse in the Second Volunteers of the U.S. Army.

"Private Thompson" continued to do hospital work until March 1862, when "he" was reassigned to carry mail for the regiment. In a letter to a friend, Sarah described in great detail, an accident she suffered while a courier, carrying the mail between Washington and Centerville, Virginia. This occurred in close proximity to where the Second Battle of Bull Run (Second Battle of Manassas) was about to begin. She was forced to ride a mule after the horse she had been riding was shot out from under her and killed. "I was trying with all my might to reach Berry's Brigade before the battle commenced, and in order to do so, I took advantage of every near cut that I possibly could, by leaping fences and ditches instead of going a long way around. When I had accomplished about half the distance between Washington and Centerville, I saw a chance to cut off a mile or more, by leaving the road and taking a shortcut, which I thought best to take advantage of, but after having gone a considerable distance from the road, I found myself confronted by a very wide ditch, which I attempted to cross; but instead of leaping across it my mule reared and fell headlong into it, and I was thrown with such force against the side of the ditch, that I was stunned and unable to escape further injury from the frantic efforts of the mule to extricate himself from such an unpleasant position. There was some water, and deep mud at the bottom of the said ditch, and where the mule tried to get up, his feet stuck fast in the mud, and he would fall back and try again. Finally, he succeeded in getting out, but how long I remained there I never knew, but the first sound that struck my ear was the booming of cannon, and the first thought that flashed across my brain was the mail. On crawling out of the ditch I realized that I had sustained severe injuries. I had no use of my left lower limb. I felt sure it was broken, and the intense pain in my left side, and breast, made me feel sick and faint; while the bare thought of the undelivered mail drove me almost frantic. While my mind was thus taking in the situation, I was trying to creep towards the mule, which stood a few yards distant, patiently waiting for me. Notwithstanding my distressed condition, I at once set about readjusting the saddle and mail bags, which now hung, mud bespattered, underneath the mule's stomach; but how to get the mud off and get on the mule's back was the all-important question. But after several ineffectual attempts to remount, I finally succeeded, by making loops in a long rope halter, and fastening one end to the pummel of the saddle. I then started for the battlefield with the utmost speed that I could endure, and after extreme suffering, I reached our troops, who had not yet become engaged in action, and after delivering the mail, I went to the rear where I found Dr. Vickery, with the hospital corps and ambulance. I made no report of the accident, but simply said that I had hurt my leg and it was very painful and asked him for something to rub on it to relieve the pain." (When Sarah returned to camp, she realized her injuries were much more serious than she thought. Along with a broken leg, there were internal injuries. Fear of discovery caused her to lie low and nurse herself).

"Private Thompson" recovered after a short period of rest. In December 1862 "he" rode as an orderly to General Poe in the Battle of Fredericksburg, riding with such skill and fearlessness that "he" received commendations from the field and officers. A few months later, one of General McClellan's spies was captured and executed. "Private Thompson" volunteered for that open position. "But was I capable of filling it with honor to myself and advantage of the Federal Government? This was an important question for me to consider were I to proceed further. I did consider it thoroughly and made up my mind to accept it with all of its fearful responsibilities." Sarah studied everything that she could find on weapons, tactics, local geography, and military personalities. When interviewed for the position, "Private Thompson" so impressed the staff, the position was "his."

"Private Thompson's" first mission as a spy involved finding yet another disguise. Sarah darkened her skin with silver nitrate and was provided men's ragged clothing and a wig by the wife of a local chaplain, the only person who knew her true identity. Sarah was so successful in her transformation that the doctor she had worked for in the hospital did not even recognize her. She now posed as a slave named "Cuff" in a nearby Confederate military camp, beginning as a construction worker on the ramparts being built to counter McClellan and his troops. Sarah's hands were so blistered after the first day she convinced a fellow worker to swap jobs with her. On the second day, Sarah worked in the kitchen where her hands could heal some and she was in a much more advantageous position to collect information by eavesdropping on various conversations. She was invisible as a slave and kitchen worker, learning much about the size of the army, weapons, and morale. Sarah discovered that "Quaker guns," which were logs painted black to look like cannons, were used as decoys at Yorktown.

It wasn't long before Sarah assumed the persona of "Private Thompson" again and was assigned to perimeter guard duty and could escape back to the regiment. Once there, valuable information was delivered to the Generals, which was well received, appreciated, and used as part of their strategy for battle. "Frank Thompson" took part in the Battle of Blackburn's Ford, the First Battle of Bull Run, and in the Peninsular Campaign, the Siege of Yorktown, which raged from April to July 1862. On May 5, 1862, the regiment came under heavy fire during the Battle of Williamsburg. "Private Thompson," caught in the thick of it, picked up a discarded musket, fired with the rest of the regiment, and did whatever needed doing at the site. As the battle raged on, "he" carried the wounded on stretchers, hour after hour in the pouring rain, to the field hospital. Later that summer, "Private Thompson" returned to the role of the mail carrier and traveled through territory that was inhabited by dangerous bushwhackers. The routes were often 100 miles or longer. "Private Thompson" saw action again in the Battles of Fair Oaks and Malvern Hill. Once more, "he" did what needed doing.

Sarah reports she was present at many historic battles, such as the Battle of Antietam in September 1862, during which she was nursing a mortally wounded soldier who confessed to her he was in fact a woman in disguise. Sarah was amazed, and probably felt a great deal of kinship, as she had at least one co-conspirator in the ranks. The following is a quote from her memoir: "I listened with breathless attention to catch every sound which fell from those dying lips, the substance of which was as follows 'I can trust you and will tell you a secret. I am not what I seem but am female. I enlisted from the purest motives, and have remained undiscovered and unsuspected… I wish you to bury me with your own hands, that none may know after my death that I am other than my appearance indicates.'… I remained with her until she died, which was about an hour. Then making a grave for her under the shadow of a mulberry tree near the battlefield, apart from all the others, with the help of two of the boys detailed to bury the dead, I carried her remains to that lonely spot and gave her a soldier's burial, without coffin or shroud, only a blanket for a winding sheet. There she sleeps in that beautiful forest, where the soft southern breezes sigh mournfully through the foliage, and the little birds sing sweetly above her grave."

At Fredericksburg, on December 13, 1862, "Private Thompson" was an aide to Colonel Orlando M. Pope, where at least twice "he" undertook intelligence missions behind Confederate lines. Ironically, this time "he" was disguised as a woman! First, as an Irish peddler woman named Bridget O'Shea, selling apples and soap, then as a Black laundress. When a packet of official papers "fell" out of an officer's jacket, "he" returned to the Union Army with the information. The generals were delighted with the find and most grateful. Another time, "Private Thompson" worked as a detective in Maryland as Charles Mayberry, exposing a spy for the Confederacy. Occasionally, as they were recorded, places and disguises have been disputed, but most appear to be historically correct. When the regiment was not engaged in battle, "he" was constantly in the saddle, relaying messages, and orders from headquarters to the front lines. They referred to "Private Thompson" as a fearless soldier who was active in every battle the regiment faced.

Early in 1863, the 2nd Michigan Infantry was assigned to the Army of the Cumberland and was sent to Kentucky. "Private Thompson" contracted malaria and requested a furlough, but it was denied. Being very sick and needing medical help immediately, "he" left anyway, despite the denial.

Since she no longer had to adopt a male persona, Sarah checked herself into a private hospital in Cairo, Illinois, intending to return to military life once recovered. After her health was restored and she was feeling strong, Sarah was heading back to the front when she saw posters listing "Frank Thompson" as a deserter. This upset her very much.

"Private Thompson" was anything but a "deserter!" Rather than risk execution for desertion, Sarah decided not to return to the military. Now she could be "herself" and no longer needed a disguise. From June 1863 until the end of the war, Sarah worked as a nurse, at the United States Christian Commission in a Washington, D.C. hospital, and other hospitals for wounded soldiers in war-torn areas such as West Virginia and Virginia.

In 1864, Sarah published her memoirs, *Nurse and Spy in the Union Army*, donating the profits to various soldiers' aid groups. While working at a hospital at Harper's Ferry in Virginia, she encountered a widower from New Brunswick, a mechanic, Linus Seelye. Much to their surprise, they discovered they had been friends as children in Canada. A courtship began soon after their initial meeting. On April 27, 1867, Sarah and Linus were married at the Wendell House Hotel in Cleveland, Ohio, and moved back to Canada. They soon returned to the United States, where they traveled across the country looking for work in Michigan, Ohio, Texas, Illinois, Louisiana, and Kansas. They had three children, all of whom died of illness in their youth. They adopted two boys from an orphanage in Louisiana that Sarah was running in the late 1870s.

In 1876, Sarah attended a reunion of the 2nd Michigan Infantry and was overwhelmingly and warmly greeted by her fellow soldiers from McClellan's Volunteers. Still very upset by her status as a "deserter," Sarah's comrades banded together to assist her in having the charge of desertion removed from her military records and did all they could to support her application for a military pension. They petitioned the War Department for a full review of her case. Finally, in 1884, after an eight-year battle, "Private Thompson" was cleared of all charges of desertion, receiving an honorable discharge. Sarah was also awarded a government pension for military service of $12 per month. In 1897 Sarah Emma Edmonds was admitted into the Grand Army of the Republic, the only woman to become a member.

Sarah was inducted into the Military Intelligence Hall of Fame in 1998.

Note: Some historians doubt Sarah's stories and suspect she may have embellished the truth to sell more copies of her memoir. According to the book *The Mysterious Private Thompson* by Laura Gansler: "The most dramatic parts of her book were her stories of espionage: the first trip behind enemy lines at Yorktown, her exploits while dressed as an Irish peddler woman, her successful reconnaissance while disguised as a female slave during the Second Battle of Bull Run, and her dramatic escape from the Confederate cavalry in Kentucky. These stories were and still are, impossible to verify, but true or not, they added a great deal of drama to her book and are the source of the enduring popular belief that Sarah was a spy. There are also events that could not have happened to her because they documented her to be somewhere else. For example, Sarah's regiment was not at Antietam, yet she wrote about being there and even included a melodramatic story of the dying woman soldier, so similar to Clara Barton's experience, which Sarah may have heard or read. Sarah also wrote about the siege at Vicksburg, which occurred several months after she left the army, as though she had been present. It is possible, however, that the source for that material was (her friend) Jerome Robbins, who had been there and may have written to Sarah about it."

Suggestions for further reading:

Nurse and Spy in the Union Army During the American Civil War by Sarah Emma Evelyn Edmonds

Behind Rebel Lines: The Incredible Story of Sarah Emma Edmonds, Civil War Spy by Seymour Reit

A Call to Arms: The Civil War Adventures of Sarah Emma Edmonds, alias Private Frank Thompson by P. G. Nagle

Sara Josephine Baker
"Dr. Jo"

"The way to keep people from dying from disease, it struck me suddenly, was to keep them from falling ill. Healthy people don't die. It sounds like a completely witless remark, but at that time it was a startling idea. Preventative medicine had hardly been born yet and had no promotion in public health work."

Sara Josephine Baker was born on November 15, 1873, in Poughkeepsie, New York. No, this is not the Sara Baker that is known and loved as an entertainer, activist, expatriate, exotic dancer, sultry singer, and French Resistance agent. That is another very interesting woman born Freda Josephine McDonald in St. Louis, Missouri, in 1906. This Josephine Baker is another story entirely.

Our Sara Josephine Baker is unique also, for different reasons. Her mother, Jenny Harwood Brown, was one of the first graduates of Vassar College. Her Father, Orlando Daniel Mosher Baker, was an attorney. He was extremely intelligent and very disciplined, but most of his education he got on his own. Sara had two sisters, Arvilla who died in infancy, Mary who lived to be twelve, and a brother, Robert Nelson Millerd Baker, who died at thirteen.

They were an affluent Quaker family and Sara recalls a happy childhood and an excellent relationship with both of her parents, living a life of privilege. "Our domestic circle had an unusual stability during all my years at home… I remember Bridget, the cook, Mary, the maid, Mrs. Unlack, the laundress and Frances, our colored nurse of blessed memory, were with us always. Frances was our other mother and my love for and understanding of the colored race date back to her and all she meant to us children. It was a good world that I lived in."

Sara's Aunt Abby, who was actually her father's aunt, was just one of a very large old-fashioned family, but certainly the most outstanding member. Sara remembers her, at nearly 100 years of age, as "a tiny old lady in severe Quaker gray with a white kerchief about her neck and her bonnet strings tied underneath her chin in a great gray bow." Aunt Abby both encouraged and challenged Josephine intellectually and instilled in her the courage to be a nonconformist. Abby said she was old enough to see things as they are, not to believe all the claptrap that society forced upon them, and certainly not to believe everything that she heard or read. Abby absolutely lived life on her own terms and encouraged Sara and her siblings to do the same thing. She would not be told what to do by anyone! Aunt Abby had a strange habit of turning things a bit upside down, of turning day into night. For example, she got up and had her breakfast at midnight, ate dinner when the sun was coming up over the horizon, took her supper at 11 a.m., then went to bed again around noon. This may sound a little like a fictional story for children, but it is in fact true. Sara and her siblings knew about these eccentricities and used to spend as many "waking" hours as possible visiting with her. Abby read stories to them from the Bible with great earnestness, never wearing spectacles as she had keen eyesight. When finished, she would close the book and in a loud whisper tell them, "Now, children, that is a very silly story. I am an old, old lady and I want all of you to remember what I am saying. It is a silly story and there is not a word of truth in it. Don't let anyone tell you that stories like that are true," then she would call her maid, "Jane! Cookies!" They had cookies and milk. Their parents never knew, nor did they think Abby odd, they just figured that she was an old lady and slept a lot both night and day. Little did they know!

Sara was certainly loved and supported by her family. Her siblings taunted her because their dad had wanted a boy but got Sara instead. Sara attempted to make up for it by idolizing him and following him everywhere. Sara loved being with her dad, and he seemed to enjoy her company as well. Even though she was a girl, he taught her to fish, row a boat, and ice fish in the winter. When Sara's little brother did finally arrive, dad was thrilled and "Jo" welcomed him into the family, becoming the "big brother," teaching Robert all the things her father had taught her. Sara recalls being schooled in proper womanly arts as well, sharing these thoughts; "I was thoroughly trained in the business of being a woman. My sister Mary and I went through rigorous education in cooking and sewing; no superficial bowing acquaintance with cookstove and sewing machine, but real work." She admits she did not like cooking, but she could still produce a meal fine enough that it was up to her dad's standards, and that was saying something!

Sara always had a tender and caring heart. I think her own words illustrate this so beautifully: "My impulse to try to do things about hopeless situations appears to have cropped out first when I was about six years old. It should be pointed out that the method I used was characteristically direct. I was all dressed up for some great occasion and (I wore) a beautiful white lacy dress with a blue sash and light blue stockings and light blue goatskin shoes. And (I was) very vain about it. While waiting for mother to come down, I wandered out in front of the house to admire myself, hoping that someone would come along and see me in all my glory. Presently, (someone) did arrive; a little, colored girl about my size. But (she was) thin and hungry looking wearing only a ragged old dress the color of ashes. I have never seen such dumb envy in any human being's face before or since. I could not stand it. It struck me right over the heart. I could not bear the idea that I had so much and she had so little. So I got down and took off every stitch I had on, right down to the blue shoes that were the joy of my (young) heart. (I) gave everything, underwear and all, to that little Black girl. I watched her as she scampered away, absolutely choked with bliss. Then I walked back into the house, completely naked (I was) wondering why I had done it and how to explain (it). Oddly enough, both father and mother seemed to understand pretty well what had gone on in my mind. They were fine people, my father, and mother."

There was the expectation that Sara would attend college, to which she was totally amenable. At age sixteen, she was excitedly preparing to study at her mother's alma mater, Vassar. She was a conventional daughter of a Victorian family. As a teenager, she enjoyed the ordinary activities of girls her age. She was completing studies at Misses Thomas' School for Young Ladies in Poughkeepsie, run by two older women who encouraged students to ask questions and think for themselves, critically, much like Aunt Abby. There were no actual grades issued, and they organized the girls into study groups so they could study what interested them. Of course, they were all required to demonstrate proficiency in all the required subjects. It was just that they did it in their own time and in their own way. Sara absolutely loved school and was one of the best students.

Sara's life was shattered when her father and younger brother suddenly died of typhoid. During this time in history, there were no water treatment plants or indoor plumbing. They pumped drinking water directly out of the Hudson River. The Baker family lived downstream from a hospital that discharged waste right into that same river. This hospital had many people suffering from typhoid. With the loss of both her father and brother and her sister Mary just the year before, Sara felt an enormous sadness and a sense of responsibility to help care for the remaining family, including financially. She was also very depressed. This was clearly a turning point in her young life. She decided to become a medical doctor, which she felt would help people and put her in a secure position as well.

She gave up a Vassar scholarship, resulting in the family strongly opposing her decision. Although many of them had more liberal views, they were still skeptical of women in the medical profession. Society deemed it unnatural and unseemly for a woman to even consider medicine as a profession. This was a time in history when there were very few women physicians and society still did not accept that it was a career path for women.

Perhaps her Aunt Abby's words echoed in her heart and mind. Sara finally persuaded her mother that, despite the odds, it was the best decision for her. Jenny must have recognized her daughter's passion and determination. In Sara's own words, "When I encountered only argument and disapproval, my native stubbornness made me decide to study medicine at all costs and in spite of everyone."

In May 1849, a New York paper *The National Era* reported that Elizabeth Blackwell graduated from medical school. "Some of our male readers may be astonished to see an M.D. attached to the name of one of the gentler sex," the editors wrote, "but we hope the time will come when an American woman, at least, can follow any honorable professional occupation... without exciting the surprise of anyone." Dr. Elizabeth Blackwell was the first female physician to practice medicine in New York. She may have been the first woman in the U.S. to graduate from medical school, but her achievement barely opened the doors of the medical profession to women. Dr. Blackwell found herself blocked from practicing at any hospital or clinic in New York City.

Sara studied chemistry and biology at home, rather than enrolling in a college course to save the tuition fees. Then she enrolled in the New York Infirmary Medical College, a medical school for women, founded by the physicians and sisters Elizabeth Blackwell and Emily Blackwell. She took full advantage of the opportunity to work with a network of very successful female physicians, including Mary Putnam Jacobi; physician, writer, suffragist, and advocate for integrating clinical and laboratory studies. The only class that gave her any difficulty was "The Normal Child" which was taught by Dr. Anne Daniel, a physician, and public health reformer. It led to her fascination and, some might say, obsession with children and their health and development. Sara graduated second in her class.

In 1898, Sara began a yearlong internship at the New England Hospital for Women and Children in Boston, Massachusetts, where she worked at an outpatient clinic in one of Boston's worst neighborhoods serving some of the city's poorest residents. While in Boston, she almost killed a drunk man as he was beating his pregnant wife, who was in labor. Sara was trying to deliver their baby. She forcibly ejected him from the apartment, and he fell down a few flights of stairs. She barricaded the door and delivered the baby. It was only when leaving, she realized with great relief, that she had not killed the brute. Working here was another education for her where she learned the harsh realities of sickness and death in those slums. It was during this year that she really came to understand the connection between poverty and ill health, which would be her focus for her entire career. "The way to keep people from dying from disease, it struck me suddenly, was to keep them from falling ill. Healthy people don't die."

Sara returned to New York and in 1899 opened a medical practice with a classmate, Dr. Florence M. Laighton. They struggled to make ends meet, earning only $185 in their first year. Women doctors were such a rarity that they had few patients. Those they had were quite happy though. Nevertheless, the practice was not thriving. I cannot imagine how frustrated Sara must have felt after all her hard work. She jumped through all the hoops. She studied, and made excellent grades, only to have doors shut in her face. Sara was broke and desperate to earn some money to support herself. To help generate additional income and cover costs in the practice, she and Dr. Leighton worked as medical examiners for the New York Life Insurance Company, paving the way for women physicians to work in the insurance industry. To apply her medical education, she opened her own clinic for impoverished women. Later, she joined with two other women doctors to expand the clinic, creating the New York Infirmary for Women and Children.

Sara also took a position as a part-time medical inspector for the city. She noticed that most of her male colleagues collected their salaries, simply filled out paperwork, and did little else. She recalled that their offices "reeked of negligence and stale tobacco smoke and slacking." Despite the adverse conditions, she was captivated by and very dedicated to the work. It was here that she met many key health administration officials. Sara quite impressed them, and rightfully so. It must have offered at least a small measure of assurance to her, finally recognized as a qualified professional. In 1907, she was appointed the assistant commissioner of health.

In this position, Sara managed smallpox vaccination programs and sanitation issues. She really loved the work and now knew, without a doubt, public health was the field where she belonged. During the 1800s and early 1900s, preventative medicine was almost unheard of. The focus was on illness, not preventing it. Infectious diseases were a major concern for both medical doctors and researchers.

In large cities, such as Boston or New York, sanitation was virtually non-existent. Horses died and were left to rot in the streets. In those same streets, they sold unpasteurized milk from open, rusty cans. Typhoid, smallpox, and dysentery were rampant. These diseases were prevalent among the young. One-third of the deaths in New York City alone were of infants, and children under the age of one year. In New York's Hell's Kitchen, near the docks of Manhattan's West Side, 15,000 infants died each week in 1902, primarily because of dysentery.

There were no public health nurses and few public health programs or policies. Female physicians were rare, and they accounted for less than one percent of all the physicians in the U.S. In general, medical schools were simply not open to women.

It was in New York City, at the turn of the century, that Dr. Jo began her life's work with the New York Department of Health as a medical inspector. To succeed in the male-dominated world of public health administration, Sara minimized her femininity, at least in her appearance. She wore masculine tailored suits with ties and joked that her colleagues sometimes forgot that she was a woman. Her first assignment was examining children in public schools. She was allotted one hour for every three schools and was to send home any child who was sick. Unfortunately, the truant officer would ultimately send those same sick children back to school! She knew this would not work. She trained school nurses and established a city-wide school nurse program that was so successful that cases of head lice and eye infections, which had plagued schools for so long, hovered around zero. Now, she took those nurses that she trained one step further. The public health nurses were going to be put to another test. She realized that with the extreme rates of infant mortality, something must be done. The idea of prevention was unheard of, but Dr. Jo knew it was the answer, and she persisted.

In 1908, Sara was appointed the head of the newly established Bureau of Child Hygiene. She was the first woman in the United States to hold an executive position in a health department. She dug in and pioneered an experiment that was wildly successful in dramatically reducing the infant mortality rates in some of the worst slums in New York. She appointed nurses to visit the mothers of newborns to provide hygiene instruction, insistence on and support for breastfeeding, check for sufficient ventilation, encourage frequent bathing, teach them about the best clothing for hot weather and outdoor airing, and discourage hazardous practices such as feeding the baby beer or allowing him or her to play in the gutter. As soon as a child was born, his or her name and address got reported to the Health Department. Dr. Jo reasoned that if they properly taught every new mother how to feed and care for a baby, and to recognize the signs of illness, the mother would have a much better chance of keeping the child alive and maybe even healthy. Sara also introduced the concept of prenatal care to prevent infant mortality during pregnancy and immediately following childbirth. This was revolutionary and clearly demonstrated the power of health education to effect real and sustained change. Sara developed a variety of programs that helped further reduce infant mortality. One of those programs was the education and licensing of midwives, which would weed out those who were practicing, but incompetent.

In 1912, Dr. A. Whitridge Williams characterized most physicians practicing obstetrics as being "incompetent and likely causing more harm, and sometimes, death, to mothers and children," many more than they attributed to midwives. After Dr. Williams' lecture, Dr. Jo realized midwives might just be the answer for best maternal and infant care, but they were not conventionally educated, regulated, or supervised. This was not the best practice by any means. She set up programs for the education and licensure of midwives. This was designed to ensure Midwives would be fully trained in medical procedures, antiseptic practice, and other areas necessary for safe childbirth, at an accredited medical facility. Only then would they receive a license. These measures alone saw the infant mortality rate drop by over fifty percent from 1907 to 1923.

Sara revolutionized pediatric health care in the United States and in other nations as well. Another of her daring projects was the establishment of "milk stations" throughout the city. Commercial milk at the time was often contaminated or mixed with chalky water to improve color and maximize profits. Dr. Jo, as she was now being called by her patients and co-workers, invented an infant formula made from water, calcium carbonate, lactose, and cow's milk. It allowed mothers the ability to go to work to support their families, and still offer a nutritious formula to their babies. These "milk stations" were locations where nurses examined babies, advised mothers, dispensed low-cost, high-quality milk, and scheduled regular checkups. Statistics show that fifteen milk stations prevented over 1,000 deaths. Forty new stations opened in 1912. In just three years, the infant death rate in New York City fell by forty percent. In December 1911, The New York Times hailed the city as the healthiest in the world.

Dr. Jo was unstoppable. She instituted a "Little Mothers League" to train young girls to care for babies. Many mothers had to work, and they put young girls in charge of caring for their younger siblings with no preparation or much instruction. Nurses taught the schoolgirls about feeding, exercising, dressing, handling, and general care of infants.

In an era when reliable birth control was unavailable and abortion was unsafe, as well as illegal, there were hundreds of newborns abandoned each year in New York City. Babies turned up in parks and alleyways or on the doorsteps of fashionable houses. Most ended up in squalid municipal almshouses with paupers, drunks, and the insane; nearly all of them died. In 1915, a foundling hospital opened on Randall's Island under the direction of Baker's Bureau of Child Hygiene. Trained nurses provided babies with state-of-the-art care and feeding. Close to half of them still died. In what Dr. Jo's nurses referred to as the "hopeless ward," where the most premature, sickly babies lay in tiny boxes lined with cotton wool, virtually none survived. They simply died of loneliness.

This intrigued and deeply upset Dr. Jo. She realized babies needed to receive tactile stimulation, to be touched, and be physically held, cuddled, and cooed to. It was really just common sense in the end. She boarded out the sickliest newborns in the hopeless ward to a corps of gushing Italian mothers on the Lower East Side who were trained in childcare by the bureau's visiting nurses. "Offhand, it sounds like murder," Dr. Jo confessed. "Moving these poor little potential ghosts out of this ward where everything was light and sterile and spic and span, into tenement rooms on Hester and Orchard streets." The results were really astonishing! They cut the death rate of these vulnerable and fragile little babies in half. "Sometimes," she wrote, "it really looked as if a baby brought up in a dingy tenement room had a better chance to survive its first year, given reasonable care, than a baby born with a silver spoon in its mouth and taken care of by a trained nurse who knew all the latest hygienic answers." The medical opinion held that mothers should train their babies early to be independent by feeding them at regular intervals and ignoring their cries and babbles. Doing otherwise was thought to damage them psychologically. We now know the opposite is true. Dr. Jo certainly acknowledged this as a truth that we now take for granted. Emotionally sensitive and responsive human contact is essential for normal child development. Without such care, children may be physically stunted, mentally disabled, or even die. Although she was a woman who never had her own children, Dr. Jo had an uncanny sense of their needs.

Next, Dr. Jo was given the worst assignment imaginable, that of reducing the death rate in Hell's Kitchen, one of the very worst slums in New York City. Maybe she was assigned this task because she was a woman, but Dr. Jo embraced the work with dedication and enthusiasm, immersing herself in caring for families amid the extreme poverty, filth, and grime. Among these rat-infested buildings, which were crammed full of immigrants, she found her stride. Jacob Riis, the photo essayist, describes it as, "a world of foul smells, scooting rats, ash barrels, dead goats, and little boys drinking beer out of milk cartons." Dr. Jo went from door to door, tenement building to tenement building, seeking people with infectious diseases.

Hell's Kitchen is a neighborhood on the West Side of Midtown Manhattan in New York City, bordered by 34th Street (or 41st Street) to the south, 59th Street to the north, 8th Avenue to the east, and the Hudson River to the west. Until the 1970s, Hell's Kitchen was a bastion of poor and working-class Irish Americans. Some memories from various publications state that, in the 1860s, the Manhattan neighborhood was a beastly wonderland of stenches, bloody parades, and diseases guaranteeing a horrible death. Among its meatpacking-focused highlights were slaughterhouses, gut cleansing, and fat boiling outfits, towering manure heaps, and stables devoted to the production of "swill milk"—the milk of frequently diseased cows that was consumed by the poor, to their detriment. There was a pork packing outfit on 39th street where blood and liquid offal flowed for two blocks before emptying into the river. During the hot summer weather, there was an extremely offensive odor of decomposition. Gutters ran with blood and filth, constantly contaminating the atmosphere. Fat boiling and gut cleansing establishments emitted gas and smoke from the chimneys that winds carried for miles. Thousands of loads of manure were dumped here in heaps to rot. The stench of these piles was intolerable. Dead animals, in various stages of decomposition, floated down the river. Crowded, poorly vented tenement houses where families tried to live surrounded this entire area. It was no small wonder that fever, cholera, dysentery, and infant deaths abounded. There were establishments that produced swill milk. *The New York Times* described it as a "filthy, bluish substance milked from cows tied up in crowded stables adjoining city distilleries and fed the hot alcoholic mash left from making whiskey. This too was doctored with plaster of Paris to take away the blueness, starch, and eggs to thicken it and molasses to give it the buttercup hue of honest Orange County milk." Back when people were drinking the stuff, reported the Times, it probably killed 8,000 children a year. This is what families in this neighborhood had to feed their children. One shudders when attempting to comprehend human beings living there. Dr. Jo noted that "I climbed stair after stair, knocked on door after door, met drunk after drunk, filthy mother after filthy mother, dying baby after dying baby." One day she had to defend herself by literally kicking yet another drunk husband down a flight of stairs as she was attempting to tend a sick woman.

Over 4,500 people in the district died weekly of cholera, dysentery, smallpox, typhoid, or some other illness. One third of them were infants. Dr. Jo rolled up her sleeves and got to work. She had discovered through her visitations that babies wrapped up in tight, restrictive clothing were dying from the heat and accidental suffocation. Dr. Jo designed baby clothing that allowed a baby room to move, and was light and comfortable, with an opening down the front. It became very popular quickly. McCall's Pattern Company bought the design and paid her a penny royalty for each one they sold. The Metropolitan Life Insurance Company was quite impressed and ordered twenty thousand copies of the pattern and distributed them to their policyholders.

Another battle that Dr. Jo fought was the silver nitrate battle. Babies at delivery routinely received silver nitrate drops in their eyes to prevent blindness caused by gonorrhea. The bottles of solution, however, often became contaminated or evaporated, leaving the concentration of silver nitrate dangerously high, causing the very blindness that it was meant to prevent. Once again, Dr. Jo showed her resourcefulness by inventing a foolproof sanitary solution. She used beeswax capsules, each holding just enough solution for one eye. They could not become contaminated as the contents were well sealed and thus could not evaporate. Soon the method was used around the world and the rate of blindness among infants dropped significantly.

After U.S. involvement in World War I, Dr. Jo became even better known. This was largely because of a statement she made to a reporter from the New York Times who had requested an interview. She told him it was "six times safer to be a soldier in the trenches of France than to be a baby born in the United States. "Soldiers are dying at a rate of four percent, whereas babies in the United States are dying at the rate of twelve percent." Her statements were both alarming and persuasive. Sara started a school lunch program for children, due to the publicity that her comments brought. She also made good use of the publicity around the high rate of young men being declared ineligible for the draft because of poor health, as a motivating factor to support her in her mission to improve the health of children.

Among Dr. Jo's many other accomplishments was a school inspection system, including the collection, organization, streamlining, and upkeep of records and procedures for public health departments, much of which was adopted across the nation. She implemented a plan to create the Federal Children's Bureau and planned to create a division of child hygiene in every state.

Dr. Jo became quite famous, albeit for a brief period, when capturing the notorious "Typhoid Mary." True story. Mary Mallon was an Irish emigre who worked as a cook and was desperate to support herself and keep her position as a cook. Mary was the first known "healthy carrier" of the disease, typhoid, although she herself suffered no ill effects, but had infected multiple households where she worked. Mary managed repeatedly to elude the authorities and unwittingly caused a small typhoid epidemic in the city. They sent Dr. Jo to the house where Mary worked to collect a medical sample for analysis. When Dr. Jo approached her to explain what she wanted, the cook charged her and attempted to stab her with a fork, then simply disappeared. Dr. Jo and a team of police officers searched for over five hours to find her. Finally, they got lucky and discovered Mary hiding in a closet. According to Dr. Jo, Mallon "came out fighting and swearing, both of which she could do with appalling efficiency and vigor." They got her in the ambulance, but Dr. Jo "literally sat on her all the way to the hospital."

Articles about Dr. Jo's lifesaving campaigns appeared in newspapers from Oklahoma to Michigan to California. In the late 1910s, she and other reformers drafted a bill to create a nationwide network of home-visiting programs, and maternal and child health clinics, modeled on the programs in New York. But the American Medical Association (AMA), backed by powerful Republicans, averse to spending money on social welfare, claimed the program was tantamount to Bolshevism. Dr. Jo was in Washington the day a young New England doctor explained the AMA's position to a congressional committee: "We oppose this bill because, if you are going to save the lives of all these women and children at public expense, what inducement will there be for young men to study medicine?" Senator Sheppard, the chairman, stiffened and leaned forward: "Perhaps I didn't understand you correctly. You surely don't mean that you want women and children to die unnecessarily or live in constant danger of sickness so there will be something for young doctors to do?" "Why not?" said the New England doctor, who did at least have the courage to admit the issue: "That's the will of God, isn't it?"

In 1915, New York University (NYU) invited Dr. Jo to lecture on child hygiene for an alternative course that led to a Ph.D. in public health. Since her prior training did not actually include a degree in public health, she agreed to teach the course in return for the opportunity to earn the diploma. Dr. William Park turned the request down flat, saying that they did not admit women. She refused the position! Park searched in vain for over a year, hoping to find a male instructor who could match Sara's training, qualifications, and experience. He failed dismally in that endeavor and finally gave up, realizing she was the one who was imminently qualified. He admitted not only Dr. Jo but also other women to the program. Now, she happily accepted the post. The reception she received from some of the male students was hostile, but she continued teaching there for fifteen years. She graduated with a degree in public health and her focus was clearly on child and infant health and wellbeing.

Dr. Jo was also an avid believer in suffrage for women and campaigned vigorously. Along with five other women, she founded the College Equal Suffrage League at NYU, an organization that campaigned for women's voting rights, and she marched in the first annual Fifth Avenue suffrage parade. She was the U.S. representative on the health committee of the League of Nations from 1922 to 1924 and was appointed consulting director in maternity and child hygiene of the U.S. Children's Bureau. Dr. Jo served a term as president of the American Medical Women's Association. After her retirement, she continued to serve on twenty-five committees that were devoted to improving children's health care. Her work clearly laid the foundation for preventative health procedures that saved hundreds of thousands of babies, which resulted in improving infant mortality rates from one in six in 1907, to one in twenty by 1943. (The current infant mortality rate for the U.S. in 2021 is 5.614 deaths per 1,000 live births, a 1.18 percent decline from 2020. The infant mortality rate for the U.S. in 2020 was 5.681 deaths per 1,000 live births, a 1.17 percent decline from 2019.)

Dr. Jo lectured throughout the United States on child hygiene and published five popular books on the subject and over two 250 magazine articles. Her fight against the damage that widespread urban poverty and ignorance caused to children, especially newborns, is perhaps her most lasting legacy.

Dr. Jo retired in 1923 and lived with the novelist and scriptwriter, I.A.R. (Ida) Wylie, who was from Australia. Dr. Jo ran their household and wrote her autobiography, *Fighting for Life*. Wylie was the author of more than a dozen romantic novels, many of which were adapted for film, including Torch Son with Joan Crawford and Keeper of the Flame with Spencer Tracy. Some have noted a similarity in tone and phrasing between Dr. Jo's writing and Wylie's, suggesting that perhaps Wylie helped her write her autobiography. Beyond that memoir, little is known of Dr. Josephine Baker's private life, as she seems to have destroyed all her personal papers.

In 1935, four years before the memoir was published, Dr. Jo and Ida moved to Princeton, New Jersey to live with another woman physician, Dr. Louise Pierce, a Rockefeller University scientist who was instrumental in finding a cure for sleeping sickness. Dr. Pierce traveled to the Belgian Congo to test it in 1922.

Note: While Dr. Jo was the prime mover, the catalyst, and often the idea person behind much of what she accomplished in her lifetime, she had help, it was a team effort. She did not bring about the necessary and wonderful change single-handedly. In her book *Fighting for Life*, Dr. Joe speaks very humbly and clearly about the many colleagues, the many hands, hearts, and minds who pitched in and helped her to see great social change and great strides in public health during her lifetime. She was a remarkably creative, caring, brilliant, and visionary woman that must be remembered.

Suggestions for further reading:

Fighting for Life (New York Review Books Classics) by S. Josephine Baker and Helen Epstein

Sarah Breedlove Walker, Madam C.J. Walker

"I had to make my own living and my own opportunity. But I made it! Don't sit down and wait for the opportunities to come. Get up and make them."

Sarah Breedlove was born on December 23, 1867, in Delta, Louisiana. She was one of six children born to Owen and Minerva (Anderson) Breedlove, enslaved on Robert W. Burney's Madison Parish plantation before the Civil War. Sarah was the first child in her family to be born into freedom after President Lincoln signed the Emancipation Proclamation on January 1, 1863. Her siblings were an older sister, Louvenia, and four brothers: Alexander, James, Solomon, and Owen Jr. In 1872, her mother died, probably from cholera. Her father remarried, but he died within a few years.

Orphaned at seven, she was sent to live with her sister Louvenia and her brother-in-law, Willie Powell, who forced her to work in the fields and wash clothes to earn her keep. She picked cotton and worked as a domestic. While few records exist, Sarah described this period of her life in many speeches and interviews. At the tender age of fourteen, she married Moses McWilliams, most likely to escape not only her oppressive working environment with her sister but also the frequent mistreatment at the hands of her brother-in-law, whom she said was "cruel." She married Moses, who worked as a laborer, in order "to get a home of my own." On June 5, 1885, she gave birth to a daughter, Lelia. Moses died two years later. The cause of his death is unknown, and records are scarce and incomplete.

Sarah's brothers had established themselves as barbers in St. Louis, Missouri. Sarah and Lelia joined them there, where Sarah found work as a washerwoman, earning $1.50 a day. It was hard work and not enough money for her to get by on. Her daughter attended public school, which was segregated at the time.

In her community, the St. Paul African Methodist Episcopal Church provided for newcomers and offered many educational resources. Sarah, always eager to learn, attended night classes whenever she could. She was also a member of the church choir and the missionary society. There were many learned and successful black men and women in the congregation. She found this uplifting and reassuring. The congregation mentored and inspired her, some of these women were members of the National Association of Colored Women and in leadership roles at the AME Church. Booker T.

Washington urged all black people to lift themselves up by developing skills, working hard, and being of excellent character. This sparked something in Sarah, who once told a reporter that she had only three months of formal education. It wasn't until 1889, at age twenty-two, that she learned to read. Sarah had dreams of a better life for her daughter and for herself. When Lelia completed the eighth grade in St. Louis, her proud and loving mother sent her to Knoxville College, where she attended advanced-level classes.

In 1894, Sarah married her second husband, John Davis. He turned out to be a lout, an all-around scoundrel, as well as a very heavy drinker. She left him around 1903 when she was thirty-seven years old.

During the 1904 World's Fair in St. Louis, Sarah attended a meeting of the National Association of Colored Women and was very impressed with the beautiful and dignified Margaret Washington, wife of Booker T. Washington, and other well-educated and civic-minded women. Sarah took more notice of her own appearance. If she looked better, she would be more confident. Her clothes were always clean, she had a sense of style, and lovely skin, but she was quite concerned about her hair. The stress in her life to this point, and her inadequate diet, had left her scalp patchy and her hair thinning and broken. It was a common ailment of many Black women of this era, but few spoke of it. They suffered severe dandruff and hair loss. Sarah concluded these conditions were due to skin disorders caused by the application of harsh products, such as lye, that were ingredients in shampoos, and laundry soap. Other factors included the infrequent ability to bathe and shampoo their hair because most Americans lacked indoor plumbing, central heat, and electricity. Sarah resolved to try different commercial products to see if she could get some relief. None worked. After giving the hair situation much thought, Sarah created a hair product for herself. This would allow her not only to solve her own hair and scalp issues, but she could start a cottage industry and help other women.

Sarah learned about hair care from her brothers, who were barbers in Saint Louis. In 1904 Sarah worked for Anne Turnbo Malone, who was an African

American hair care specialist and owner of The Poro Company.

On July 21, 1905, Sarah and her daughter moved to Denver, Colorado, where she not only continued to sell products for Malone but also worked as a cook for a pharmacist, who assisted her in refining her formula until it achieved the results she was looking for. Physicians and pharmacists used the basic formula to remedy skin ailments. She experimented a bit, and after some trial and error and many false starts, three of her formulas met her criteria; Wonderful Hair Grower, Vegetable Shampoo, and Glossine. She marketed them using before and after pictures of herself as a model. She was now proud of her healthy tresses, which were beautiful because of her products.

Sarah had a friend in St. Louis with whom she kept in communication after she moved. His name was Charles Joseph Walker, a newspaper man who also sold advertising. He traveled to Denver, and in a romantic gesture, asked for her hand in marriage. They married on January 4, 1906. This is when Sarah became "Madam C.J. Walker." She took

Charles' name and the "Madam," from the French pioneers in the beauty industry. Lelia also took Walker as her surname. Charles, known as C.J., was Sarah's husband, and her business partner, providing invaluable advice and direction on advertising and promotion for her fledgling company. Sarah marketed herself as an independent hairdresser and inventor of hair care products.

In the beginning, Sarah operated out of her own home to guarantee a reliable water source for shampooing her customer's hair properly. The *Denver Statesman* displayed ads that gave the hours of operation of her shop. Her products earned her upwards of $10 per week. Sarah put her daughter Lelia in charge of the growing mail order business in Denver, while she and Charles traveled throughout the U.S. to expand the business.

In 1908, Madam Walker and her husband moved to Pittsburgh, Pennsylvania. They opened Lelia College, which was a training school whereupon graduating, students earned a certificate as a "hair culturist." When Madam Walker and C.J. moved to Indianapolis in February 1910, Lelia took over the day-to-day operations in Pittsburgh. The site in Indianapolis soon became the new headquarters for the Madam C. J. Walker Manufacturing Company.

Before long, Lelia persuaded her mother to establish yet another office and salon in Harlem, New York, which she did in 1913. The business was booming. They purchased a house in downtown Indianapolis where she later built a factory, beauty school, and hair salon, as well as a school to train her agents, and a laboratory to help with research. She sought and hired a very competent staff that included attorneys Freeman B. Ransom and Robert Lee Brokenburr, factory manager Alice Kelly and educator Marjorie Stewart Joyner, among others, to help guide the growing and very successful company. Most of the company's employees, including key management positions, were women.

Now, with a 3,000-person powerful sales force, motivated by commission, Sarah was one of the largest employers of African American women whom she carefully vetted, groomed, and trained. Besides training her women in sales and grooming, Sarah instructed and encouraged other Black women to become independent through budgeting and building their own businesses. At her national conventions, she rewarded them for their charitable deeds by giving out prizes to women who had aided their local communities. Sarah's company was successful beyond her wildest imagination. During 1908, sales reached $6,672 and would soon hit $250,000. While the businesses continued to grow, Sarah and C.J. grew apart. They separated and divorced in 1912.

Madam Walker personally demonstrated the products she was so proud of in schools, churches, and many other public places. She took elocution and penmanship lessons. With her striking persona, fine clothing, and a "can do" attitude, along with her electric car, she made quite an impressive figure. By 1920, her product market expanded beyond the United States to Cuba, Jamaica, Haiti, Panama, Costa Rica, and Europe. "At a time when unskilled white workers earned about $11 per week, Madam Walker's agents were making $5 to $15 per day, pioneering a system of multilevel marketing that Walker and her associates perfected for the black market," wrote Harvard professor Henry Louis Gates Jr. in a 1998 story for *TIME* magazine. It was 1916 and Lelia, now thirty-one was living in Harlem and managing the business.

There was a sharp increase in demand for Madam Walker's products since Lelia moved to Harlem. She urged her mother to join her there. Madam, who was desirous of a more progressive political environment, as she had become rather political, acquiesced. Her health was also failing, and Lelia urged her mother, to no avail, to travel less. When Madam moved to Harlem, the mother and daughter team reveled in fraternizing with figures who would also become larger than life. Figures like Ida B. Wells. W.E.B. DuBois was often a guest in their home. Lelia hosted salons featuring other writers like Langston Hughes and Zora Neale Hurston.

Madam took on leadership roles in the NAACP, joining the executive committee of the New York Chapter, and helped to organize the 1917 Silent Protest Parade. Madam was active in the community, and Lelia, who was tall and gorgeous, was dubbed "goddess of the Harlem Renaissance." In his memoir, *The Big Sea*, penned in 1940, Langston Hughes called Lelia "the joy goddess of Harlem's 1920s."

Madam and Lelia were local celebrities living the dream, in a spectacular townhouse on 136th Street near Lenox Avenue.

In 1917 Madam began searching for a weekend estate where she could entertain. One realtor suggested a 3-acre plot of land in Irvington, which was an elite, all-white neighborhood known for grand mansions and exclusivity. He suggested that this neighborhood is absolutely where you want to be to make a statement. Apparently, she liked the statement she was making. Sarah hired Vertner Tandy, the first licensed Black architect in New York State. He had overseen the construction of the four-story Harlem townhouse where she currently lived. Tandy built Sarah's new manse, Villa Lewaro, located on the Hudson River, in Westchester County, New York.

Tandy designed a glorious three-storied stucco villa with a terrace that led to a swimming pool. The interior had very high ceilings, many tall windows, a grand marble staircase, and lovely hardwood floors. The Italian Renaissance architecture influenced his design. She accomplished all of this for $250,000, at the time quite a fortune. They installed an Estey organ in the ornate music room. Estey, the esteemed Vermont organ maker, was very reticent about sending employees to build and install this organ when they found out that Madam Walker was a woman of color. Estey questioned how this woman could know of such things and how she would pay for them, but in the end, they did it. Madam was familiar with the grand organ because St. Paul AME Church had installed a Kilgen organ in its new church during the 1890s. The cost of the Estey was $25,000. Her music room was where Broadway composer John Rosamond Johnson and Frederick Douglass' grandson, Joseph Douglass, a violinist, all performed. Madam never learned to play a musical instrument, but she was a powerful supporter and patron of the arts. She had been exposed to a wide variety of music that ranged from ragtime to German lieder to opera and sacred music. Her church organist and choir director back in St. Louis was an African American man who was classically trained as a tenor and who had performed an opera at the Chicago World's Fair in 1893.

Madam Walker did not let fame and fortune make her greedy. She was a philanthropist who generously shared her wealth, helping to raise funds. She pledged $1,000 personally, to support the building of a new facility at a branch of the Young Men's Christian Association (YMCA) in Indianapolis's black community, pledging further funding for other YMCAs. She contributed scholarship funds to the Tuskegee Institute, Flanner House, and Bethel African Methodist Episcopal Church in Indianapolis, Mary McLeod Bethune's Daytona Education and Industrial School for Negro Girls (later known as Bethune-Cookman University in Florida), the Palmer Memorial Institute in North Carolina, Haines Normal School and Industrial Institute in Georgia, Preservation of Frederick Douglas's Anacostia House in Washington D.C., and the NAACP, specifically the anti-lynching fund. She also bequeathed large amounts of money to schools, old age homes, and universities. Perhaps the best thing Madam C.J. Walker left in the world was her story and legacy as an enduring role model for future generations.

Sarah was truly an inspiration for all, but particularly for young African American women who faced more struggles than most. In keeping with her philanthropy and generous support of the arts, Madam envisioned the Walker Building before her death in 1919. When it finally opened in 1927, in Indianapolis, Indiana, it housed her corporate offices and a factory. As an African American cultural center for decades, it is now a registered and preserved National Historic Landmark. It was renamed the Madam Walker Theatre Center. It is a 944-seat theater, featuring an Egyptian and Moroccan motif. At one time, it housed a drugstore, a restaurant, the Walker factory (organizational and professional offices), and a barbershop. Today, it is still a cultural arts center and continues to house organizational and professional offices, including a beauty salon. She once said, "I am a woman who came from the cotton fields of the South. From there, I was promoted to the washtub. From there I was promoted to the cook kitchen. And from there, I promoted myself into the business of manufacturing hair goods and preparations. I have built my own factory on my own ground." Her will stipulated that one-third of her company was to be left to her daughter, Leila, and the rest to charity.

In 1998, the U.S. Postal Service issued a stamp of Madam C.J. Walker as part of its "Black Heritage" series.

Since the first writing of this book, PBS has broadcast a mini-series, 'Self-Made' Story of American Millionaire, Madam C.J. Walker.

Suggestions for further reading:

On Her Own Ground: The Life and Times of Madam C.J. Walker by A'Lelia Bundles

Madam C. J. Walker (21st Century Skills Library: Life Skills Biographies) by Katie Marsico

Madam C.J. Walker: Entrepreneur (Black Americans of Achievement) by A'Lelia Bundles

Madam C.J. Walker (Gateway Biographies) by Penny Colman

Madeleine Zabriskie Doty

"I packed my bags with a beating heart. Go I
would - for why life unless adventure?"

Madeleine Zabriskie Doty was born on August 24, 1877, in Bayonne, New Jersey. Her parents were Samuel William Doty and Charlotte Gautier Zabriskie Doty. They had three children: Madeleine, Douglas, and Ralph. Madeleine earned a B.L. (Bachelor of Law) from Smith College in 1900 and studied law at Harvard, even though women were strictly barred. Madeleine attended four lectures dressed as a man. She wore a tailored suit and a hat hiding her hair, but a professor discovered her and called her out. She argued her case before the faculty but was not allowed to continue. It is appalling so many women have been forced to assume a male persona to succeed in their chosen path. Yet, we must applaud their free thinking and hutzpah!

In 1902, Madeleine earned her L.L.B. (Bachelor of Laws), from New York University, graduating at the top of her class. After practicing law for five years in New York City, she focused on the children's courts, delinquency, and social reform work. For three years Madeleine was secretary of the Russell Sage Foundation Children's Court Committee, working in the juvenile court system until 1912 when she was appointed to the New York State Commission on

Prison Reform. This began her long career in public service.

Madeleine was among the few early female lawyers. In 1870, the U.S. census noted five women lawyers. In 1900, there were 108 lawyers and judges in the U.S., the great majority of whom were white men. Only 1,010 were women. By 1950, the number of female attorneys had increased, though women remain in the minority and often experienced pay disparity.

Madeleine was a determined feminist and reformer, accepting some extreme challenges to promote the change she envisioned. Her experiences during her education fanned those flames. In 1913, a scant year into her new position with the state, she decided that the best way to determine what reforms they needed in the prison system was to become a prisoner! With the cooperation of the warden and the chief matron, they incarcerated her for four days as "Maggie Martin" in the women's penitentiary at Auburn on a fabricated charge of forgery. Here it is again, hutzpah!

Upon her release, Madeleine wrote a scathing exposé for the New York Sunday Post, describing the deplorable conditions and the poor treatment she received as a prisoner. This experience compelled her to write *Society's Misfits* (1916), about juvenile and women's prison reform. Her goal was to see change, and Madeleine wanted to make it happen.

Madeleine attended the Women's Peace Congress in 1915 at the Hague, along with forty-three other women from the United States. She was an ardent pacifist, and a member of an international circle of other pacifist women, becoming a correspondent for the *New York Tribune* and *Good Housekeeping.*

When World War II broke out, Madeleine's world came tumbling down around her like so many sandcastles. She questioned her work for prison reform when the entire world seemed on fire. How could she keep her focus? Where could she put her energy and talent now?

In 1916, while Madeleine was in Germany, reporting the effects of war on the poor, she visited a friend at the American Embassy in Berlin. He advised her to leave, saying that her presence would make trouble for them at the embassy. "I shall… break no rules, cause no trouble, but I'm in search of the truth, and as a free American citizen I mean to talk to everyone I can from the Kaiser to Liebknecht," (a peace activist who was very vocal). Madeleine's friend warned her she would be watched constantly by the authorities and watched they were! In one of her musings, she wrote: "The funny thing about German spies is that they dress for the part. They are as unmistakable as Sherlock Holmes. They nearly always wear gray clothes, a soft gray hat, are pale-faced, shifty-eyed, smooth-shaven, or have only a slight mustache, and carry canes."

Madeleine spoke no German, but her friend and traveling companion spoke the language fluently. Together they gave the spies a chase throughout Berlin. "We jumped from one car to another. It proved an exciting game. Once we went up to a gray-clad man and asked him if he wasn't tired. But spies grow angry when spoken to. German officials have no sense of humor. If they had, I wonder if there would have been a war." This escapade provided great comic relief, eliminating some stress and tension.

Being followed eventually lost its charm and wasn't fun anymore. Madeleine wrote: "I feel exactly as though I am in prison. I acquire the habit of looking out of the corner of my eye and over my shoulder. These spies are as annoying to their countrymen as to me. The people detest them. They grow restless under such suppression. Free conversation is impossible, except behind closed doors..."

At age forty, Madeleine traveled to Russia as a correspondent for the *New York Tribune* and *Good Housekeeping*, covering the Bolshevik revolution. She provided an eyewitness account for the American public. Madeleine spent six weeks in Petrograd and observed firsthand this tumultuous period in Russian history. By 1917, most people in Petrograd (now St. Petersburg) had lost faith in the Tsarist regime. Government corruption was unrestrained, and Tsar Nicholas II disregarded the Imperial Duma. Thousands of workers flooded the streets of Petrograd to show their dissatisfaction. On March 8 of the same year, demonstrators clamoring for bread took to the streets in the Russian capital of Petrograd. Supported by ninety men and women on strike, the protesters clashed with police but refused to leave the streets.

Madeleine had arrived not only to this chaos and fermenting uprising, but also it was the dead of winter. She experienced illness and poverty in very hostile surroundings and had no access to medical care. When she found a doctor, he had no medications because the chemists were on strike. Madeleine was a virtual prisoner again, this time in a hotel, and not of her choosing. The streets were filled with revolutionary tensions, causing her great anxiety. The revolution impacted all aspects of daily life for everyone, including Madeleine. She relied on the housemaid for friendship and help. "I lay and shivered and waited for street fighting to begin. When the machine guns opened fire, what should I do? If the soldiers entered to search for loot, would they spare me? How was I to explain that I was an American, a worker, not a capitalist?"

When Madeleine regained a modicum of health and felt somewhat at ease, she could more fully appreciate her surroundings and focus on the issues she had come to cover. Madeleine interviewed deposed ministers of the former government that were imprisoned in dire conditions; witnessed the trials of the Revolutionary Tribunal that had replaced all the judges and lawyers overnight, befriended Maxim Gorky, who tried to help the Russian people and condemned the Bolsheviks. Alexei Maximovich Peshkov, known as Maxim Gorky, was a Russian writer and political activist. He was nominated five times for the Nobel Prize in literature.

Madeleine listened to people talking as she rode the train through Siberia. She penned the article titled "Revolutionary Justice," published in the *Atlantic*: "The working class had risen. The extreme left of the Socialists, the Bolsheviks, had gained control... overturning the Provisional Government under Kerensky, which had failed in providing what the working people wanted - peace, bread, and land."

After returning to a more conventional life, Madeleine had a serious love affair with the noted author, David Graham Phillips. He was an American journalist and novelist, whose interests ranged from the plight of women to corruption in Congress. Late in 1918, she was engaged to Roger Nash Baldwin, an educator, social worker, probation officer, and pacifist who did not believe in war. Roger was one of the founders of the American Civil Liberties Union. As a conscientious objector, he served a year in prison for refusing the draft.

Roger and Madeleine were married in August 1919 and lived in Greenwich Village until 1924. Madeleine was selected as the International Secretary of the Women's League for Peace and Freedom in Geneva, Switzerland, then as editor of Pax International for the League of Nations. From this point on, she spent most of her life abroad with occasional visits to New York and Florida. This must have put undue stress on the marriage. They amicably divorced in 1925.

Madeleine created the first Geneva Junior Year Abroad Program for the University of Delaware. She returned to academia and earned her Ph.D. in International Relations from the University of Geneva in 1934. She was sixty-six years old.

In 1946 Madeleine came back to the United States and organized another Geneva Junior Year Abroad Program for her alma mater, Smith College, running the program there for three years. The program continues today and is a living legacy for this brave, forward-thinking, and rather indomitable woman.

In 1950, Madeleine taught history at Miss Harris' School in Florida. The warmer climate appealed to her. When she retired from this position at age seventy-five, she was still feeling the fire of reform. She returned to Geneva, becoming a lecturer at the University. In 1962 she retired at last, settling in Greenfield, Massachusetts. Madeleine published several books: *Society's Misfits* (1916) on juvenile and women's prison reform; *Short Rations: An American Woman in Germany* (1917); and *Behind the Battle Line* (1918).

Suggestions for further reading:

One Woman Determined to Make a Difference: The Life of Madeleine Zabriskie Doty by Madeleine Z. Doty and Alice Duffy Rinehart

Short Rations: An American Woman in Germany, 1915-1916 (Classic Reprint) by Madeleine Zabriskie Doty

Behind the Battle Line: Around the World in 1918 by
Madeleine Zabriskie Doty

In Conclusion

Each one of these women had vision, belief in themselves, courage, and persistence. Each of us has our own vision and gifts. To live a life that is authentic and meaningful, we must identify those gifts and use them. Sometimes we just need a little help. Role models can offer us help if we know them. We all need role models to inspire and guide us! Because history is predominantly written by the victors, history books reflect their creators' assumptions about whose history is valuable. For much of the Western world, this means that the perspectives and stories of wealthy white men dominate our histories. We have not seriously considered the history of women to be of much value, and consequently, it is often left unrecorded. Multicultural women are even more grossly overlooked in mainstream history. Ruth Bader Ginsburg said, "Women belong in all the places decisions are being made." She didn't specify race, color, creed, or sexual preference.

When we recognize the achievements of all women, in every facet of life, not just the "womanly arts," there is a large impact on the development of self-esteem and self-respect for girls and women. We see women in government, community, literature, medicine, law, sports, science, politics, the arts, and everywhere else! Boys and men will also benefit from the elimination of stereotypes. It allows women and girls to be viewed as equals, rather than the "weaker sex." Knowing the women who went before us enables us to find new ways to walk our paths with pride and confidence. That was the driving force behind my desire to write this book.

These women continue to inspire me, and I hope they inspire you as well. We must recognize women as leaders and the influential force they are in our society and always have been. When we reframe history, we see not only the dignity and accomplishments of women, but their bravery, integrity, and passion. They were not all just subservient handmaidens. It is necessary to rethink the old cliches about women. We must not focus on the oppression and negativity of the patriarchy that has held women captive for so long. Together we can break those old chains of patriarchal rule and focus on new ways of being in the world. It begins with knowledge, acceptance, and then action.

In telling women's stories, we become aware of how the patriarchy, and many cultural expectations, cause significant damage. Fortunately, this damage can be repaired--awareness is the first step. When we know the stories of our foremothers, whether familial or universal, our choices are better informed. Women's history is not a sub-category, nor is it an afterthought. Women's history is the story of humanity; women are half the population and hold up half the sky.

Made in the USA
Columbia, SC
06 March 2023